SEVEN PILLARS OF SALES SUCCESS

Jonathan Evetts

Foreword by Og Mandino

EVETTS SALES SYSTEMS
44 PRIMROSE HILL ROAD
RHINEBECK, NEW YORK 12572
914-876-6827
FAX 914-876-3332

 Sterling Publishing Co., Inc.   New York

DEDICATION

This book is dedicated to the fond memory of my father Harold Edward Evetts, from whom I learned many of the selling principles it contains, and to my mother Helen, who instilled in me a love of literature and a lifelong ambition to write.

Library of Congress Cataloging-in-Publication Data

Evetts, Jonathan.
    Seven pillars of sales success / Jonathan Evetts ; foreword by Og Mandino.
        p.   cm.
    ISBN 0-8069-7204-1
    1. Selling.   2. Success in business.   I. Title.
    HF5438.25.E94   1990
    658.8'5—dc20   89-78232
                                                              CIP

Portions of this text appeared in slightly different form in Jonathan Evetts'articles in the Nov./Dec. 1986, Jan./Feb. 1987, and May/June 1987 issues of *Personal Selling Power* and the May/June 1989 issue of *Selling Space*.

10 9 8 7 6 5 4 3 2

© 1990 by Jonathan Evetts
Published by Sterling Publishing Company, Inc.
387 Park Avenue South, New York, N.Y. 10016
Distributed in Canada by Sterling Publishing
c/o Canadian Manda Group, P.O. Box 920, Station U
Toronto, Ontario, Canada M8Z 5P9
Distributed in Great Britain and Europe by Cassell PLC
Artillery House, Artillery Row, London SW1P 1RT, England
Distributed in Australia by Capricorn Ltd.
P.O. Box 665, Lane Cove, NSW 2066
Manufactured in the United States of America
All rights reserved
Sterling ISBN 0-8069-7204-1   Paper

CONTENTS

CONTENTS 5

FOREWORD

I probably have been involved in selling, in one form or another, most of my life. As a first grader, trying to earn my own Daisy air rifle, I knocked on countless doors after school, with the latest editions of *Liberty* and *The Saturday Evening Post* that I was peddling at a nickel a copy and, not too long ago, I appeared on the *Today Show* hoping to sell their vast audience on purchasing my latest book. There is just no way for any of us to avoid getting involved in selling, whether we like it or not, and, as we approach the twenty-first century, a talented sales person will be worth far more than his or her weight in gold.

Only someone with a background as colorful and varied as Jonathan Evetts has enjoyed—and endured —could have written this very special book. His powerful pillars to sales success were not fashioned by some classroom theorist, but by a tough and wise individual who has been down in the trenches and survived the agonies of telephone "boiler rooms," door-to-door rejections, and the supreme challenge . . . motivating others, as Vice President of Sales, to exceed their performance of yesterday and last week.

It will be obvious to every reader that selling is far more than just another means of earning a living to the author. You will encounter words, phrases, and techniques in this book that rarely, if ever, have appeared before in a book on salesmanship: The Link Phenomenon, Integrity, Rapport, Good Manners, Selling Light, Memorable Selling, Ethical Value-based Selling, The Testimonial Culture, Selling Through Speaking, Selling Through Writing.

Each decade seems to produce a special sales book, perfect for its time. Whether you've been a salesperson for decades or are just a rookie trying to discover what the art of selling is all about, this is your book—the perfect guide for anyone wishing to succeed as a salesperson in the nineties. Apply its lessons and watch your income soar. I promise!

—Og Mandino
Author, *The Greatest Salesman in the World*, Parts I & II

INTRODUCTION

The United States is the land of opportunity, and selling is surely the ultimate career of opportunity in this land of opportunity.

Career sales people often take for granted financial rewards that are limited only by their capacity to produce, and the freedom to manage themselves while still enjoying all the benefits of company employment. Add these and many other rewards to work that is already demanding, exciting, and requires some very special talents, and it is easy to understand why so many professional sales people are openly enthusiastic about everything relating to selling.

In fact, this very enthusiasm often leads us to overlook the problems that are also associated with selling for a living. When asked, for instance, why our peers in other professions tend to view selling as a less than honorable career, and why so many talented people drop out or fail to make it in sales, we rarely have good answers.

Selling has been very good to me, just as it is the fast track to financial success and the highest levels of management for thousands of others, but it still has serious "image" problems. This book addresses the problems head on, and then lays out for you, in clear, easy-to-follow stages, a "lifetime selling plan," as it is derived from the ethical, logical, and business basis of the "Seven Pillars."

You will also find that the book contains many brand new selling concepts, such as "See Yourself As Others Sell You," "Tactical and Strategic Listening," and the "Secret of the Negative Shared Experience," which can be used as "sales aerobics" in breathing new life into the attitudes and techniques you bring to your customers.

If there is a category lacking among the many excellent books on selling, it is a "manual" for daily use by sales people to help them over the tough spots that inevitably occur in a world of intense competition and universal technology. The dictionary defines "pillar" as a "main support," and the "Seven Pillars" will always be there to provide support when you need them.

Prospective customers for sales training programs differ from those who are in the market for printing, diesel locomotives, or industrial chemicals, because they are quite rightly more interested in *how* rather than *what* they are sold. In other words, their attitude is, "If he can sell me this training program, then his sales system must work, and I'll 'buy' it!"

In reading this book, continuously test the methods being presented, by asking yourself: "Does it make sense?" "From my own experience, will it work?" "Is this how *I* would like to be sold?" and finally, "Am I sold, and do I buy into this way of selling for myself and my people?"

If, at the end of the book, you can give a resounding "Yes" to all these questions, and especially the last one, then you too have found your "lifetime selling plan," and can start at once to enlist the Power, Integrity and Enjoyment of the "Seven Pillars" to boost your sales success!

THE SEVEN PILLARS OF SALES SUCCESS

Enthusiasm • Honesty • Energy • High Motivation • Money-Maker • Courageous • Problem-Solver • Alert • Knowledgeable • Well-Qualified • Inspires Confidence • Good Listener • Values Customer's Own Knowledge • Attends to Detail • Good Appearance • Manages the Sale • Keeps in Touch • Brings Something New to Every Meeting • Sense of Humor • Diplomatic • Persistent • In Sync with Prospect • Good Planner • Caring • Skilled Communicator •

These are just a few of the numerous winning qualities emphasized recently by a group of successful sales professionals in describing an outstanding sales person.

But when the same people were questioned about their experiences as *customers* of real estate companies, department stores, car dealers, appliance outlets, and many other businesses, the sales people encountered by them were frequently described as: Deceitful, Liars, Pushy, Misrepresenting, Insincere, Phoney, Manipulative, Condescending, Underhanded, Insulting, Over-Familiar, and Unreliable. They were also accused of: Not Listening, Not Knowing What They Were Selling, Lack of Interest, Not Following Up, and Not Giving Good Service.

When the ideal and the actual in selling produce such an extreme dichotomy in the assessments of the same group of qualified professional observers, it is

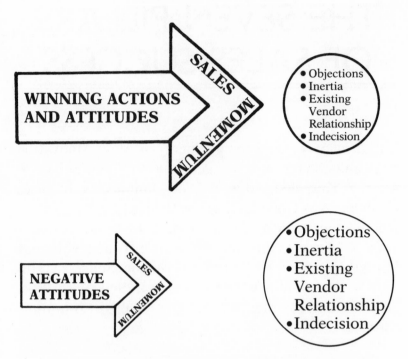

How the winning actions and attitudes of high sales achievers over-come buyer inertia and sales resistance, while negative attitudes of below-average sellers actually have the opposite effect.

surely time for a radically different approach to sales and sales training.

Selling's ancient origins are lost in the mists of human history, but only in recent years has it begun to be recognized as a science rather than as a haphazard occurrence in which luck was more important than sound professional practice. In fact, we now know so much about selling and the structure of a sale that almost anyone can be taught to sell well.

But when sales people are either not trained at all, or their training focuses only on superficial motivation and slick techniques, they are often left without the deeper values needed to see them through when the going gets tough.

The Paradox of Selling

Perhaps the greatest paradox of a sales career is that the job's main attractions—freedom, high pay, expense accounts, and free travel—can generate tensions that can damage social relationships, wreck marriages, and erode personal values. And today's intense competition, universally available technology, and price selling only tend to compound these stresses. It was not for nothing that indigestion used to be called the "Salesman's Disease."

My own original sales success was accompanied by such severe personal problems that I was forced to completely rethink and reorient all of my values and goals at a fairly early age. From the need for a "real" basis for my career and from many years of trial and error came the ideas for the "Seven Pillars of Sales Success." First-hand experience of the excitement and opportunities of selling in the United States provided a fresh perspective and the incentive to push forward with the development of an advanced sales system— one that balances ethics with achievement and benefits professional sales people everywhere.

Integrity and the "Sleaze Factor"

The Seven Pillars and their accompanying progressive selling system share a foundation of absolute integrity, and if you have been taught questionable selling practices or a variety of deceitful closes, they must all be surrendered before you can enjoy full reliance on the strength and high professionalism of the Seven Pillars.

In training situations, the contrast between such very different ways of selling is sometimes so vividly perceived that participants find themselves caught up in an enthusiastic competition for superlatives. As their old, unhappy pictures of selling are driven out by clear, positive images of the many skills and talents needed for ethical sales success, a wave of excitement will lift the whole group beyond what they can express, to a bright vision of what they too can achieve when they sell at the highest level!

This is the farthest possible distance from the situation where sales people allowed to choose their own titles are so ashamed of the "sleaze factor" associated with selling that they will pick "Account Manager," "Promotional Consultant," "Account Executive," "Applications Engineer," Marketing Representative," "Client Liaison"—in fact, anything but "Sales Person!"

Building your own Lifetime Selling Plan using the structure of the Seven Pillars is not difficult, but it does take dedication and conviction, and a steadfast desire to raise yourself above the ranks of the average in your profession. The Pillars emphasize ethics and proven values, to be applied with the help of a "Seven by Seven" Positive Action Acronym, which reduces fear of rejection and call-reluctance while building the positive self-image so essential to sales success.

Positive Action Acronym

The Acronym is really a 49-word summary of literally hundreds of powerful, positive, sales-related concepts, and is based on the seven-letter word *PILLARS*, with a Pillar for each day of the week.

Each of the words in the Seven Pillars has been care-

Components of Dynamic Sales Achievement

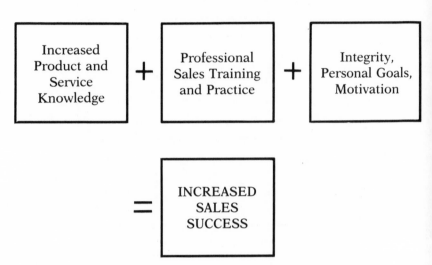

fully chosen for the effect it has had in increasing the sales (and the well-being and sales-enjoyment) of those who have used it.

The Positive Action Acronym can be used vertically, horizontally, diagonally, or even at random, to produce a virtually infinite range of permutations. The order of the Pillars, and the individual word orders, are not important, as long as they work for you. The crucial thing is that you begin right now to incorporate them into your selling. You might use one Pillar (or permutation) for each selling day. Start to visualize yourself as having all the power and winning qualities associated with the words and Pillars you are using. As you do so, long-held, hidden doubts about the true worth of what you do for a living will be replaced by the growing certainty

POSITIVE ACTION ACRONYM

PRIDE	POWER	PERSIST	PERFORM	PERSUADE	PURPOSE	PROFESSIONAL
INTEGRITY	IDEAS	INTUITION	INFORM	INTELLIGENT	IDEALS	IMPACT
LISTEN	LIKE	LOYALTY	LADDER	LOGIC	LEADER	LIFT
LEARN	LUCK	LUCRATIVE	LIMITLESS	LIAISON	LATENT	LINK
AUTHORITY	ABILITY	APPRAISE	ADVANTAGE	ACTION	ADVICE	ASSURANCE
RAPPORT	RESOURCE	REASSURE	RESOLVE	REPRESENT	RESEARCH	RESPONSE
SERVICE	SATISFY	SENSITIVE	SKILLFUL	STIMULATE	SYSTEM	SINCERITY

that you now hold the very keys to success in selling and satisfaction in life!

Powerful Affirmations

As you continue to use them, these forceful, radiating statements will grow steadily in reality and power, until they become for you a deeply gratifying way of life and a broad highway to the fulfillment of your maximum sales potential.

Here are some powerful affirmations drawn from the First Pillar, for the first day, week, or month that you will be using this new system. I stress the "day, week, or month" because some people feel the benefits of the affirmations in only one or two days, while others build their affirmative structures more gradually. In either case, it is not advisable to "push" the consciousness shift. Let it occur naturally and progressively.

First Pillar Success Statements

To be repeated three times each, thoughtfully but with vigor, and with belief in improved results. Do this last thing before you go to bed (to "set" the ideas in your subconscious overnight) and then again early in the morning.

Hold eye-contact with yourself in a mirror and repeat the First Pillar affirmations. This has the effect of sharpening the attention and increasing concentration—and of a corresponding boost in affirmation-effectiveness.

PRIDE

"I HAVE *PRIDE* IN MYSELF AS A SALES PERSON!"

"I HAVE *PRIDE* IN THE SELLING PROFESSION!"

"I AM *PROUD* OF THE MANY WAYS IN WHICH I AM ABLE TO HELP AND SERVE MY PROSPECTS AND CUSTOMERS!"

INTEGRITY

"IN SELLING, I KNOW THAT MY *INTEGRITY* IS POWER!"

"*INTEGRITY* IS MORE IMPORTANT TO ME AND MY COMPANY THAN ANY SINGLE SALE!"

"THE POWER OF MY SALES *INTEGRITY* IS ACTIVELY HELPING ME MAKE BIGGER AND MORE PROFITABLE SALES!"

LISTEN

"MY WILLING ABILITY TO *LISTEN* AND UNDERSTAND INCREASES WITH EVERY HOUR OF EVERY DAY!"

"I DO NOT FORGET TO *LISTEN*, JUST AS I DO NOT FORGET TO HELP MY CUSTOMERS!"

"NERVOUSNESS CANNOT MAKE ME TALK MORE THAN I *LISTEN*!"

LEARN

"MY WILLINGNESS TO *LEARN* CAUSES IDEAS OF PROSPERITY TO FLOW TO ME, AND THROUGH ME TO MY CUSTOMERS!"

"TO *LEARN* FROM MY CUSTOMERS IS POWER, GROWTH, AND SUCCESS FOR ME!"

"PROSPECTS AND CUSTOMERS *LEARN* AND BENEFIT FROM THE VALUABLE INFORMATION I BRING THEM!"

AUTHORITY "I HAVE FULL *AUTHORITY* TO CONTROL MY LIFE, MY SALES SUCCESS, AND EVERY ASPECT OF MY SELLING CAREER!"
"I AM A SALES PROFESSIONAL OF RECOGNIZED *AUTHORITY*, BY MY CUSTOMERS AND BY MY COMPANY!"
"MY INBORN *AUTHORITY* GIVES ME DIGNITY BUT NOT CONCEIT, CONTROL NOT ARROGANCE!"

RAPPORT "I AM ABLE TO ESTABLISH STRONG BONDS OF EMPATHY, WARMTH, AND UNDERSTANDING—TRUE *RAPPORT*—WITH EVEN THE MOST DIFFICULT CUSTOMER!"
"THIS *RAPPORT* EXTENDS TO MY FAMILY, FRIENDS, AND BUSI-NESS ASSOCIATES!"
"MY CUSTOMERS, FAMILY, AND OTHERS ALL FEEL AND BENE-FIT FROM THE GENUINE WARMTH OF THE *RAPPORT* THAT I ESTABLISH!"

SERVICE "STARTING TODAY, I WILL HOLD TO THE HIGHEST STANDARDS OF *SERVICE*, FROM MYSELF AND FROM OTHERS!"

"SERVICE IS NOT JUST A SEVEN-
LETTER WORD; IT IS A CENTRAL
CONCEPT OF MY SALES SUC-
CESS!"
"THE *SERVICE* I GLADLY GIVE
SETS ME APART FROM MY COM-
PETITORS AND GUARANTEES
MY SALES SUCCESS!"

Read the power-affirmations of the First Pillar aloud to yourself and I will almost guarantee that you will feel a sudden surge of energy—an infusion of confidence in your ability to rise above present limitations and to achieve your unbounded aspirations.

The Affirmations are even more effective when you design them yourself, so use the ones given here as models to construct your own affirmations from the other word-pillars in the Positive Action Acronym or from any of hundreds of other positive expressions.

The Pillars have just one purpose: To increase your sales and your prosperity and the prosperity of your customers. They have been designed to meet the individual needs of all who use them. So don't be restricted by the words and permutations of word-order of the Acronym, but continually inject fresh life into it by substituting other words that work for you, and in any order you please.

Selling Is _____ a Serious Business

Before delving into detailed sales techniques and the different stages of the sale, I want to ask you to examine your own personal attitude to selling. So many people who have been trained to be pleasant to customers do so without ever putting their hearts into it because of their inner dislike of selling and because they regard it as a very serious business. The truth is that selling is one of the pleasantest ways imaginable to spend your working life.

Selling is the art of making friends, of helping people, and of having fun—all rolled into one. So right now, change the title of this section to read Selling Is *Not* a Serious Business!—and then set out to prove it.

The Art and Science of Selling

So-called "natural" sales people practiced the art of selling for thousands of years before it was recognized as being also a science. These "naturals" have always sold bigger orders more often, from their intuitive knowledge of exactly what to do at all times. But don't give up if you're not one of them because mastering the science of selling will open your mind to the art as well. For each sales star who is born, thousands can attain stardom through training and practice. The basic training rules for rapid improvement are: first, Train; second, Motivate; third, Support. When these three educative requirements are met, sales people have no good reason not to succeed.

See Yourself As Others Sell You

To jump-start your advanced sales training, begin at once to "see yourself as others *sell* you." From now on, every time you buy, closely observe and analyze the actions and approach of those who sell to you. Ask yourself: "Are they selling according to a logical plan?" "What stage have they reached?" "How well are they doing?" "In their place, how would I do it better?"

Seeing yourself as others sell you will immediately start to sharpen your appreciation of the sales process, and with it your own sales skills. It will change your selling perspective from negative or neutral to positive. It is one of the simplest and most effective of all selling-improvement exercises.

The Seven Steps to the Sale

Although your Attitude, Motivation, and Ethics are all embodied in the Seven Pillars, and are inseparable

See Yourself As Others Sell You

- Is this a logical selling method?
- What stage has seller reached?
- How well is seller doing?
- **How would I do it better?**

from lasting achievement, they must still be combined with the Seven Logical Sales Steps for ultimate selling success.

Right and Left Brain Selling

The Pillars allow you to master the Art, and the Steps, the Science, of selling, and each complements the other. The Art is Right Brain/Intuitive; the Science, Left

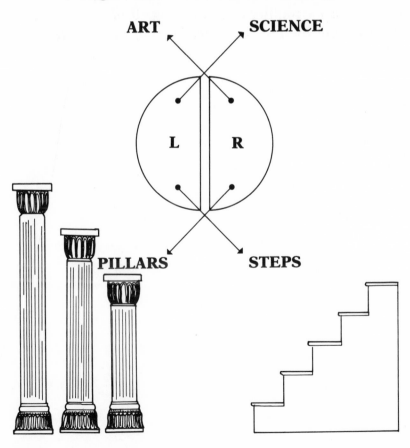

Brain/Rational, which means that the Pillars may be used at random, but the Steps must always be taken in their logical sequence of: LINK/RAPPORT/ APPRAISE/DEMONSTRATE/VERIFY/AGREE/ CLOSE.

Winning Actions and Attitudes

At the end of each chapter WINNING ACTIONS AND ATTITUDES will summarize the sales-building actions you need to take before going further. With the possible exception of designing your own Pillars, none of these actions requires any writing. Rather, they are entertaining mental energizers for you to practice as you sell.

THE FIRST PILLAR/
THE FIRST STEP
LINK

Definition: Connect, Join, Unite, Bridge.
Key Affirmation: "I am *proud* of the many ways in which I am able to help my prospects and customers!"
Approximate Length of Step: 15 to 45 seconds.
Key Actions: Comment 50 percent/listen 50 percent.
Key Attitudes: Move from stranger to acquaintance to helping friend. Go out to make friends and help others.

First-Contact Difficulties

Linking is the first, often the shortest, and possibly the most difficult stage of the sale. It covers those moments of initial contact, when time can seem to stand still as we search desperately for the right words to say—moments that have been called the "toughest thirty seconds of selling."

"If I can just talk to someone for a few minutes, I'm okay," sales people will say, "it's just getting started that I find so difficult . . ." To sales managers, who are well acquainted with problems of "getting started," this is like saying that selling is terrific, except for having to approach strangers and ask for orders. What else do they need sales people for?

"Link" Stress Level

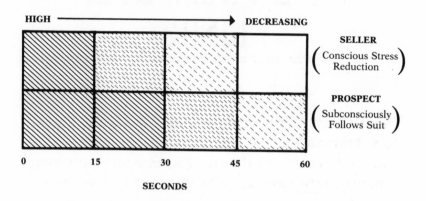

Riddle of the Approaching Stranger

Never forget that a million years of social conditioning stand between two people meeting for the first time, and this makes any fear, mistrust, or embarrassment seem quite natural. After all, the African raised-palm greeting and our own handshake survive as evidence of primitive man's need to show that his right hand concealed no weapon, and his heart no evil intent.

As you approach prospects for the first time, all of their five senses and their intuition are collaborating to register clear-cut first impressions of your appearance, the sound of your voice, and the quality of your handshake. Do prospects take note of such details of dress and behavior and measure their findings against their stored profile of what they have learned to look for in someone worth buying from? Albert Mehrabian's UCLA research showing that communications effectiveness is 55 percent dependent on body language offers strong evidence that enduring impressions are formed without a word being spoken.

For instance, sales people who mar an otherwise good appearance by wearing dirty shoes don't realize that in neglecting a seemingly insignificant detail of their "appearance package," they are alerting prospects and customers to a potential carelessness about important-order details.

More Than a Hearty Handshake

That some sales people can have problems with something as simple as shaking hands is illustrated by the experience of a Chinese-American sales rep in Los Angeles. This man had been born in China, where the handshake is not part of the culture, and after moving to Southern California, had found work in the warehouse of a prominent manufacturer's agent there. Hard work and persistence soon won him a chance in outside sales, where his eagerness to justify the promotion found him working longer hours than anyone else, and even making urgent deliveries to customers in his own car on weekends.

But no matter how hard he tried, sales in the territory kept falling off until the agency owner was forced to step in. He visited several large distributors to find out what was wrong, and heard nothing but praise for the new man's attitude, product-knowledge, appearance, and service—until an outspoken sales manager blurted out that his sales people strongly objected to the rep's limp, unpleasant, boneless handshake. Orders

Approaching Stranger

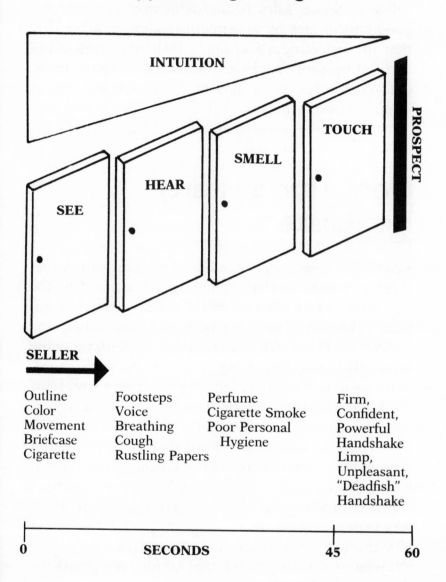

INTUITION

PROSPECT

TOUCH

SMELL

HEAR

SEE

SELLER

Outline	Footsteps	Perfume	Firm,
Color	Voice	Cigarette Smoke	Confident,
Movement	Breathing	Poor Personal	Powerful
Briefcase	Cough	Hygiene	Handshake
Cigarette	Rustling Papers		Limp, Unpleasant, "Deadfish" Handshake

0   SECONDS   45   60

were falling off because they wouldn't make calls with the rep, for fear that their customers would react in the same way.

Determined not to lose an outstanding employee, but knowing that something had to be done, the owner enlisted the help of his other sales people. The result was a novel "handshake clinic" at the next sales meeting, which included corrective hints—not just for the new rep—but for anyone rated by his peers at less than nine on a handshake scale of one to ten.

The Chinese-American rep went on to a partnership in the agency, and to far more selling success with his customers than could be credited to his new, improved handshake.

Sales women often mention their fear of having a hand crushed by some baboon who gets pleasure from seeing other people wince, and men are not immune to nervousness on this same score. Until you know if a prospect has a civilized handshake, follow the politicians' and surgeons' practice of holding the fingers straight, and not fully engaging your hand with the other person's. This makes for a less easily damaged, more flexible hand structure. After all, if it works for Queen Elizabeth II, it will work for you too!

At this point, you may be saying to yourself, "So what! Who cares about this handshaking stuff?"—even though this is probably the only physical contact you will have with your customer. The first moments of customer contact are moments of vital first impressions, and someone with hot, sticky palms or a grasp like a dead fish will be remembered for that long after their other more pleasant aspects have been forgotten.

"What Do I Say?"

For most sales people, however, Linking is not so much
a problem of appearance or handshakes as it is of finding opening words that don't sound self-conscious or
insincere. Their concerns are summed up in the frequent questions: "What do I say to someone I've never
met before?" and "How do I avoid sounding phoney
when opening the conversation?"

The answers lie in keeping it simple and keeping it
natural. All you really need are a few questions on a
variety of topics with which to prime prospects' conversational pumps, and your reputation as someone
who is both interesting and interested in others will
spread rapidly.

Unlike Rapport-building, which follows Linking and
is usually concerned with prospects' immediate business and personal surroundings, Linking relates to
broader, more objective, and less personal environments. Some of the most effective Linkers use spare
moments to read a broad range of publications and to
stay tuned to the local radio news, and it is from these
wider spheres that their Linking phrases come. They
develop a detailed knowledge of their customers' general environments—weather, traffic, crime, entertainment, business—allowing them to speak from actual
shared experience instead of tentative, hoped-for common interests.

Secret of the Negative Shared Experience

Paradoxically, for a meeting wherein the eventual aim
is a positive outcome in the form of an order, negative
shared experiences often make the best Linking ma-

terial. Positive experiences—a beautiful day or a winning sports team—call into play shallow emotions that are poor deflectors of fear and suspicion, and may even cost you control of the meeting, as prospects are distracted by their own enthusiasm. The negative shared experience furnishes far better Linking material, because it is the ordinary difficulties of life—bad weather, strikes, traffic problems—that unite the minds of strangers in sympathy and a search for solutions.

A "traffic" Link: "They really need to find a better way to handle these presidential visits, instead of gridlocking the whole city. . . . The radio said that it was even worse over on your side than it was near me."

This is an open-ended, rhetorical question on a topic of immediate interest that shows genuine concern for the other person's difficulties, while Linking them to your own. A good example of a negative shared experience will stimulate comments by prospects almost as a reflex, and in so doing serve as a potent fear-deflector. Its negative nature ensures that the response will still be reasonably brief and controlled.

A "weather" Link: "Boy! That fog was awful this morning. I was delayed almost an hour coming in. . . . I do hope that you didn't have too much trouble getting to work?"

This Link possesses the same negative qualities, and, for those who enjoy taking risks, offers the chance for a little brinkmanship.

Cliff-Hanging

When the prospect responds with his or her traffic or weather "war story," let your expression register genuine sympathy, and then offer to help by rescheduling the meeting. As Linking material this ploy has few

equals. It completely dissolves residual fear and dis-
trust, and actually stimulates buying interest, as you
demonstrate an unselfish willingness to step back from
the sale. Of the hundreds of times that I have made
this offer, it has never once backfired, but the risk that
it might adds spice to selling.

Names and Spectacles

Linking is always most effective when sales people tailor questions to individual personalities and surroundings, but there are two "guaranteed" Links: Names and
Spectacles.

Name Links can be used when a prospect's first, last,
or company name is unusual or hard to pronounce.
All the sales person has to do is comment that the name
is unusual and then ask how to pronounce it and what
its origins are. Prospects are always delighted to talk
about a subject of great interest to them, and incidentally one that underlines your concern with them as
individual human beings.

A New York sales woman once told me that the best
"icebreaker" she knew was to compliment people on
the design of their glasses, and then continue with
questions about where they bought them, how much
they cost, and how long it took to fill the prescription.
Skeptical about spectacles? Try this Link, and you'll
have to admit that they make a great topic, perhaps
because wearers of glasses all secretly long to be told
that they look attractive in them.

The Link Phenomenon

The need to Link when you sell is something of a modern phenomenon, an outgrowth of a fast-moving so-

ciety that constantly throws strangers together and of the paranoia and suspicion bred in customers by the sheer numbers of suppliers competing for their business.

Initial rudeness on the part of prospects needs to be seen for what it so often is: the desperate last defense of a decent human being who is constantly called upon to decide in favor of one product or sales person and not another. Give buyers the benefit of the doubt by recognizing the pressures they are under, and don't be in a hurry to take offense!

Linking recognizes the very human need for forming first impressions. It sets the scene for you to first deflect and then dissolve the natural fear and suspicion felt by a buyer on first contact with a sales person. It also works to help sales people get through those tough contact-moments, by encouraging them to focus on the other person instead of on themselves.

If fear of rejection sometimes overwhelms you at the thought of meeting unknown buyers, just remind yourself that although they don't have to buy, they'd like to hear of how you can help them.

Five Minutes Early

Success and failure in selling are separated only by small, incremental differences in attitude and technique. Always arriving five minutes early for appointments is a good example of one of these differences.

Far from being a waste of time, early arrival lets you pause before going in—to fill your thoughts with positive Seven Pillar affirmations and with this clear statement: "I am the best thing that can happen to [use prospect's name] today!" And add, "What I sell will bring her/his company increased prosperity!" Then practice and hold to a confident mental attitude that makes room for an infinite number of *Yeses!* but can't find space for a single *No!*

Once you've given your name to the receptionist (and a business card for accuracy), and discovered which door the buyers use, sit where you can watch both it and the "action" in the reception area. How the receptionist interacts with staff members, customers, and other sales people, by phone and in person, tells you so much about the company that you may even decide that you don't want them for clients.

If the choice of lobby seating is only among overstuffed, oversoft chairs and sofas, into which one can sink almost without trace, sit on the arm or remain standing. There is no worse first impression than that conveyed by a sales person struggling up from the depths of a chair to greet a buyer who is impatiently waiting to shake hands with and guide that person to his office.

Arriving early encourages a "shift" from your world to that of the prospect, and allows you to scan the industry magazines in the lobby. These contain an update on every topic of urgent business interest to your contact, and glancing through them will make you current—and help you to appear alert and knowledgeable from the start of the meeting. They may also yield some excellent "needs" questions that you would not otherwise have thought of. The quickest way to extract information in the few minutes available is to read the contents list, and then flip through the magazine from back to front, scanning for items of interest.

"How Long Do I Wait?"

Put three sales people together in a waiting area, and one will inevitably ask the others how long they allow customers to keep them waiting. The dilemma is obvious: Wait too long, and you show how little you value your time and self-esteem; leave too soon, and you could ruin a budding relationship and lose an order. But both these concerns neglect the more important one of maintaining control of the sales relationship.

Every case has to be decided on its merits, but generally wait no longer than fifteen minutes for someone who reneges on a firm appointment. Having arrived early (to Link and develop Rapport with the receptionist), check again at the precise meeting time to confirm that the person knows you're there. Communications can go awry, and it is self-destructive to retreat into a sales-blocking fury about being kept waiting when your contact may be sitting on the other side of the same partition cursing you for being late because no one told him you were there.

Whatever the temptations, maintain your selling orientation by staying cool, objective, and focussed on the customer and not on yourself.

At five minutes after time, ask if the person will be able to see you today, and given an affirmative answer, wait another five minutes. Then make it clear that you very much want to meet with your contact (even ask to speak to the person by inter-office phone), but that you have other appointments to keep. Five minutes more, and you ask to reschedule the meeting, as you have to leave. This takes a little nerve, but for every unthinking, inconsiderate client who objects, there are many more who will respect your professionalism.

When a prospect subjects you to endless phone calls during a meeting, consider that someone who makes an appointment, only to accept or even initiate phone calls throughout the meeting, may not be a person with whom you want to do business. Leaving after a pre-decided grace period is one way to handle such gross discourtesy. At the same time, when prospects use telephone interruptions to demonstrate their power over you, there is a lot to be said for just good-humoredly waiting the talker out.

Forget You Met Them on the Phone

If you're one of the millions of sales people who use the telephone to make appointments to sell in person, don't fall into the trap that so many of them do and assume that because you've talked to prospects on the phone, you needn't bother to Link on initial face-to-face contact. Work instead on the assumption that they don't clearly remember what you've said, and that there are considerable comprehension-voids about your company and its services.

Just because sales people are enthusiastic about what they sell and are concerned about keeping appointments doesn't mean that prospects share those concerns. You and your success are matters of indifference to them, and this is confirmed by the fact of phone calls that have made little impression on them. Counter this indifference by taking special care with the "in person" Link, and treating the early steps of the sale as though there had been no earlier communication.

Winning Actions and Attitudes

- Use the First Pillar Affirmations for a full week.
- Read magazines, newspapers, and advertisements to enlarge your store of general information and to accumulate Linking material. Tune in to the local radio news station.
- Start now to invest yourself with an atmosphere of warmth, caring, and good humor, so that the transition to the Rapport step is easy and imperceptible.
- Rehearse Linking comments to yourself, to prepare for your next sales call.

THE SECOND PILLAR/
THE SECOND STEP
RAPPORT

Definition: Sympathy, Accord, Affinity, Empathy, Harmonious relationship.
Key Affirmation: "The increasing power of my *integrity* is helping me to make bigger and more profitable sales!"
Approximate Length of Step: 5 to 20 minutes.
Key Actions: Comment 30 percent/Listen 70 percent.
Key Attitudes: Alertness and optimism, as you project honesty, interest, and genuine concern.

"When Do I Take the Next Step?"

Intuition and observation are the best guides to knowing when to make an imperceptible transition from one step to the next. Uneasiness on this score means that the sales person is usually fixing his attention on the individual stages of the sale at the expense of the whole, and has not understood that the successive steps are only intended as a progress chart to a scientific selling process.

In advancing from Linking to Rapport, you will be looking for signs that prospects are a little less afraid of what you might do to them—are a shade more comfortable in your presence. As a chronic fear of all buyers in dealing with an unknown sales person is, "What will this person do to me?", it is well worthwhile to let them know now that in fact you are there to work with and for them.

If they are still drumming their fingers on the desk and telling you in high-pitched, hurried tones how busy they are, manage the situation by deliberately lowering the pitch and rate of your own voice until they begin to follow suit.

Making Yourself Known

The Rapport step is your first and best opportunity to make your personal qualities known to prospects— before telling them about your company and its products. It also lets you replace any lingering suspicions with a selling atmosphere of relaxed trust.

Sales are often lost at this early stage in the meeting, when sellers rush to promote products before the still-fragile communications bridge is strong enough to carry the heavy verbal traffic of the sale. First, the seller must create a comfort zone within which to work with the prospect, and then begin to construct an enduring edifice of mutual respect and rapport.

Good Selling Is Just Good Manners

I like to train sales people to think of themselves as almost-perfect hosts to customers, whether at your place or theirs. Almost-perfect, because the ultimate goal is obviously not just to give them a good time, but to make a sale. In an age of bad manners that have spilled over into selling, the idea that good manners and sales success are closely related strikes some people as odd—perhaps until they hear that it is supported by no less an authority than Stanley Marcus of Neiman Marcus. A long-time sales person from that company told me recently that Mr. Marcus built sales at his stores by always encouraging his sales staff to treat customers as their guests.

An experienced hostess guarantees the success of her party by focussing her attention—not on the possibility of a flop—but on the comfort and enjoyment of her guests, and a professional sales person who adopts the same attitude to customers will always write more orders as a result.

Abstractions and Absorption

The pressures of modern life have intensified problems of abstraction and self-absorption on the parts of customers and sellers alike. It is almost as if each were living inside a clear plastic cylinder that permits unimpeded hearing, speech, and vision, but excludes all communication of feelings. Both of these cylinders must be dislodged before any real selling can be done. Sales people who ignore this problem and rush in with mouths on "automatic," to inundate buyers with facts and figures, features and benefits, are looking for trouble. They should not be surprised when they bounce right off the prospect, and even seriously damage their sale.

The knack is to manage one's self-absorption creatively, so that it actually moves the sale forward. Silence that small voice that keeps repeating, "I must make this sale, or they'll repossess my car or take away my house . . . ," and put aside personal concerns to focus on those of your prospect. This genuine personal interest quickly dissolves their introspection and allows them to enjoy the meeting too.

Heretofore, British Army defaulters in Egypt had to drill in the scorching Middle Eastern sun carrying backpacks full of sand. But those soldiers were no more heavily laden than sales people who go out every day oppressed by the idea that they *have* to sell—an attitude problem that is closely related to what I wrote earlier about having fun as you sell. Selling is *not* a serious business; instead it gives you wonderful, renewable opportunities to make friends and to help people, and there is no more enjoyable activity than that!

Drop those sixty pounds of sand, and as you forget your own worries by concentrating on the needs of your customer, fears of failure, of rejection, and of meeting strangers will all fall away with them. Ask yourself at the start of each day how someone with this golden view of selling can possibly have anything to fear? Expect to have fun and to be welcomed as you sell! Anticipate enjoying all the boundless freedom and limitless opportunities of the finest profession on earth!

Taking Control

Many prospects, and especially those who don't really know what they need, subconsciously want the seller to take control of the sale. In other words, quietly assuming the management of the meeting, will usually have a calming effect on undecided prospects and on those who exhibit continuing signs of nervousness or suspicion. Such meeting-management is never heavy-handed, but rather the barely perceptible guiding of the sale, hinted at in the following:

There is often a natural pause in the conversation, somewhere at the start of a sales call, and perhaps just after you have been asked to sit down. This can be the perfect time to take out your card. Remain standing, look the prospect in the eye, and, as you present your card, repeat your name slowly and distinctly, even if you have only recently introduced yourself.

This will leave an enduring impression of your face and name, linked to that of your company and its logo, as recipients meet your gaze and hear you identified before instinctively glancing down at the card. It also puts them at ease, by letting them address you with confidence when they may have earlier misheard your name or quickly forgotten it.

At this point, if you are not offered a card in return, ask for one. Don't do any selling until the exchange has been completed. By remaining standing, and asking for a card in return, you have begun to control the meeting at its outset and can build on this advantage to complete the sale.

When someone doesn't have a card, don't be embarrassed to ask for the same information on a piece of paper, while stressing how important correct names and titles are to you. This reassures prospects that you will be just as careful with the vital details of their orders.

Sales people who don't bother to ask for cards constantly miss chances to demonstrate

their professionalism, to control the sales encounter, and to show that they care about those
all-important details. They also forget that, to
customers, the most welcome words of all are
their own names correctly pronounced and
spelled. (From "The Art Of Presenting Your
Business Card," see Appendix 2 for the full
text.)

Particularly when selling to large companies (with
their constantly changing department names, telephone numbers, and titles), jot down a "date received"
on the card, and ask for a new one every three to six
months. Keeping up with ever-changing Centrex numbers, and reducing "screen" delays and "phone tag,"
make filing business cards well worthwhile, and this

The Art of Presenting the Business Card

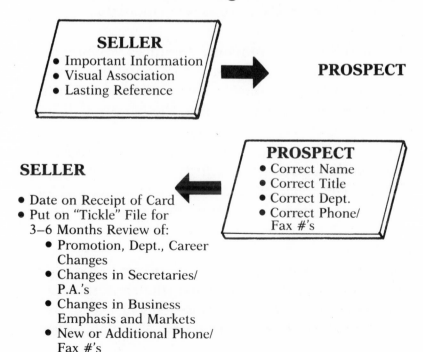

SELLER
- Important Information
- Visual Association
- Lasting Reference

PROSPECT

PROSPECT
- Correct Name
- Correct Title
- Correct Dept.
- Correct Phone/
  Fax #'s

SELLER

- Date on Receipt of Card
- Put on "Tickle" File for
  3–6 Months Review of:
    - Promotion, Dept., Career
      Changes
    - Changes in Secretaries/
      P.A.'s
    - Changes in Business
      Emphasis and Markets
    - New or Additional Phone/
      Fax #'s

ready access to accurate, current client information improves efficiency and increases sales.

The Eyes Have It

Public speaking coaches always stress the need to look into the eyes of an audience, and although selling can better be described as public listening, good eye contact is vital here too. The difference is that public speaking takes place at comfortable viewing distances, while selling often occurs close-up and face-to-face, where occular parallax interferes with strong visual interaction.

As we meet a prospect's gaze, the first few moments are easy—until our eyes take charge and start jumping from the prospect's forehead to the chin to the back wall and back to the eyes again. And to the prospect, our flickering eyeballs make us seem more than a little devious and shifty.

Dramatic actors in romantic embraces or glaring at each other in furious toe-to-toe confrontations have a simple solution to the physical impossibility of looking into both of another actor's eyes at the same time. They just choose *one* eye, and look into that. When adopted by sales people, this technique conveys to customers a relaxed directness and integrity that is appreciated by them. The single-point gaze can be maintained for long periods without any strain. Best of all, the other person can't tell that you aren't looking into both of their eyes.

Sales people will argue that they prefer to focus on another part of the face—the ear, the chin, the nose —but what can the tip of the nose tell you, except that it is red and sore? The Bible states, "The light of the body is the eye," and sustained eye-contact is as essential to reading people as reading people is to effective selling.

From Control to Questions

The "taking control functions" of exchanging business cards and establishing single-focus eye contact also round out the "social" phase of selling, during which you complete the turning of the attention of prospects from you to their own concerns.

This is done by a little questioning on the topic that fascinates everyone—themselves. The intensity of the interest that people take in their own business and social status, their family lineage, their vacations and prominent acquaintances, quickly drives out lingering vestiges of awkwardness or embarrassment, to cement a rapport that is strong enough to support this and future sales.

In contrast to Linking, which relies on experience drawn from the general or wider environment, Rapport-building uses office ornaments, plaques, awards, photographs, paintings, and potted plants belonging to immediate business surroundings. Collections of anything—hats, T-shirts, mugs, coasters, antiques—are evidence of sustained enthusiasms that rank highly as potential Rapport topics. Pictures of dogs, cats, or boats that are larger and more prominent than those of family members are clues to latent fanaticisms that you may hesitate to probe.

In asking simple, unintimidating, deeply-interested questions on a chosen topic, think of yourself as steadily extending the comfort zone within which to sell. And don't forget the physical dimensions of the "zone."

Step back after shaking hands and lean back, rather than forward, in your chair, to show sensitivity to their personal "space." This will have the effect of activating in prospects a subconscious "retention urge," or desire to keep you with them, that also raises the "perceived" value of what you have to sell. Moving away from prospects, both physically and mentally, in this way postpones decision-making pressure on them, and draws them out emotionally and intellectually.

Monkey-See, Monkey-Do

To sales people, the main value of body language lies not in the manipulation of customers but in deciphering their reactions to our selling techniques, almost before they are aware of those reactions themselves. At the first hint of negative vibes, we can rapidly adjust our thoughts, words, and actions, and get the sale back on the track and moving again, before any serious damage is done.

But some sellers are so fixated on mirroring body language that they become involved in exciting, daily games of "monkey-see, monkey-do." Let the prospect but cross her knees, and their legs are wrapped halfway around their bodies. She touches an ear, and they're stretching their lobes to their shoulders. And when she turns her head, there they are, nodding like owls on a post. It's really surprising that some alert prospect doesn't have them picked up and thrown bodily out of her office, while they're still tied in knots.

Make better use of body language by trying the 25 percent response, whereby the first negative indication is ignored as being of no consequence. Then, crossed knees elicit crossed ankles; folded arms, your hands held together in the lap; an averted face, a slight shifting in your chair. Such unobtrusive "patterning" reinforces an empathetic bond, which encourages prospects to follow suit when you return to a more "open" pose.

Selling Light

Ever asked yourself how welcome you really are at your accounts? Or if the size of your briefcase has any effect on your closing rate?

Early in my career, I repped advertising photographers on commission in London. Day after day spent phoning ad agency art directors for appointments was followed—rain, hail, or shine—by my dragging a huge, bulging portfolio and trays of slides all over London, by "tube," bus, and taxi.

After over six months without making a single sale, the idea began to dawn that something might possibly be wrong, so I took the day off to reconsider the whole situation. Out of this came a conviction that, as no one was buying anyway, whatever I did in the future couldn't be any worse.

So, having stuffed that bloated portfolio and the slide boxes into a cupboard, and researched the art director's accounts, I slipped an envelope containing a few carefully selected and absolutely superb 8 × 10 color prints into a folded copy of the London *Times*, and set out on the next call.

Surprise number one came when the ad agency receptionist took my name, and on seeing me heading for the end of a seated row of portfolio-encumbered reps, called out, "Oh! You needn't wait, Sir! You can go straight in!" Second surprise, when the art director, instead of lying back in his chair with an air of "I don't care," jumped to his feet with a broad smile and hand outstretched to greet me with a hearty, "Good Morning! How are you? Please sit down." Surprise number three, when he followed that up with, "Thank heavens you're not another blasted salesman!"

Of course, I considered the dishonest approach, but that makes for bad sales relationships, and he'd find out soon enough anyway, so instead I responded apologetically, "I . . . er . . . hate to tell you this . . . but actually I *am* another 'blasted salesman.' " "Oh!" he shot back, "I've nothing against sales people as such; it's just that they all come in here with those monstrous great sample-bags, and they talk and talk, and never listen to a word that I say!"

People facing violent death are said to see their whole lives flash instantly before their eyes, but sitting there, it was like watching an old, grainy, black-and-white newsreel of all those calls where I'd talked and talked, and never asked a single question, or listened at all.

You can guess the rest. He talked for an hour about all the reasons why he couldn't give me any work, but then, after an excellent lunch, made sure that I left with a large order tucked securely in my top pocket, and a hard-earned sales lesson clearly in mind.

A wintry sun faded into darkness, until my office was lit only by the pale glow of street lamps three stories below, as I thought and rethought what I had learned.

Obviously, researching the art director's accounts, and matching my samples to his interests and to those accounts, had paid off. And ditching that portfolio had certainly lifted a heavy physical weight that seriously limited the number of calls I could make and left me tired by lunchtime. Getting rid of it set me apart from the overloaded competition, and entirely changed the way the customer perceived me. I also saw that the portfolio had sabotaged all those earlier calls with its unspoken message, "I've got a hundred samples here, and you're going to sit there and look at every one of them before I leave!"

Going in "light" had restored the customer's absolute right to set the length of the meeting, and proved that samples didn't sell as much as the way I treated people.

But—best of all—lifting that physical load had relieved me of the crushing psychological burden of *having* to sell. From that day on, I have never gone out to sell anything. Rather I go out to make friends, to have fun, and to help people.

Those who practice the sales-killing habit of carrying with them far more than they really need are usually the same ones who have difficulty getting out of the office to make their calls. They fear rejection, suffer from severe call-reluctance, and overcompensate by carrying as much of the office with them as they can —not dreaming that this can sabotage their chances of writing orders. If you're one of them, try instead the rewards and freedom of "selling light."

Winning Actions and Attitudes

- This week, use the Second Pillar Affirmations.
- Don't rush to start selling. Reinforce the Link.
- Rise above self-absorption and the burden of having to sell.
- Assert control and establish correct eye-contact.
- Not "monkey-see, monkey-do," but the 25 percent response.
- Good selling is just good manners.
- Try selling "light."

THE THIRD PILLAR/
THE THIRD STEP
APPRAISAL

Definition: Survey, Estimate, Evaluate, Judge.
Key Affirmation: "My ability to *listen* and compre-
hend increases with every hour of every day!"
Approximate Length of Step: 10 to 30 minutes.
Key Actions: Question 25 percent/Listen 75 percent.
Key Attitudes: Reassure, support, advise, consult,
commend.

"What Exactly Am I Selling?"

Before they can help anyone, there is one question that
all sales people must ask themselves: "What exactly is
it that I am selling?" And in case you're thinking of a
quick response in terms of some product or service,
the answer is hardly ever the products or services that
your company gives you to sell.

This is well illustrated by the story of the first sales
woman for a British speciality steels company that had
previously employed only men in its sales division. She
listened respectfully to all the reasons why she couldn't
succeed in a male-dominated field, and then decided
to do something completely different.

She had a small steel bar specially finished and engraved with the company's name, and carried it with
her in a walnut presentation box. Not for her the rust-

ing, abandoned heaps of rod and scrap, as she painted vivid, verbal pictures for her customers of a beautiful, versatile metal, and then opened the walnut box to display the polished and engraved bar glowing lustrously on its blue velvet.

When the steel company executives inquired how she had quickly managed to outsell their two top salesmen combined, she said simply, "I just asked myself, 'What exactly is it that I'm selling?' "

- Knowledgeable sales trainers don't sell seminars and work books, but improved seller performance, and increased profits.
- Limousine operators stress exclusiveness, status, and convenience, not the services of an over-sized taxi-cab.
- Perfumers don't sell tiny, exorbitantly-priced bottles of scent, but glamour, romance, and dreams fulfilled.

Tangible or intangible, mundane or exciting, avoid selling a service or product—but instead look behind it for how it benefits people, for what it says to their primary buying motives of VANITY, TRANQUILITY, ENJOYMENT, or GAIN, and then sell that!

Concept Selling

Stick with this question of, "What exactly is it that I'm selling?", for when you've correctly answered it, you will know the true meaning of concept selling and will be in a position to help prospects with new insights into the concepts *they* can use to sell *their* services and products.

Shared Understanding and Knowledge Facilitate Sales

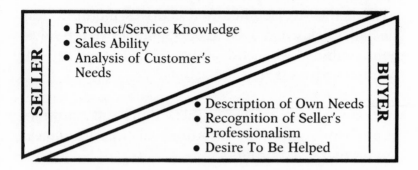

And a particularly important point: As one of the millions of American sales people who every day call prospects for appointments, be clear about what you are selling when you go telephone prospecting. On this occasion, you are selling a face-to-face *appointment* to sell what you sell.

What Are They Buying?

Put yourself in the prospect's shoes as you look for answers to the question, "What are they buying?"

Again, it is not primarily the things you carry.

People will buy from you in direct response to your success in helping them to meet their needs, in consulting with them on satisfying their wants, and in counselling them on solving their problems. The old maxim about sales people only selling what they know and understand is matched by customers who buy only when they see that you understand and care about those wants, needs, and problems of theirs. Recognize that even the most interested prospects often don't know exactly what they should buy, and that exposing their true needs is an important part of precision-questioning.

The best Appraisal questions not only showcase your professionalism, but assume that buyers generally only talk to new suppliers because of dissatisfaction with an old one. This definitely doesn't mean open season for knocking competitors, which is always a mistake, but that some questions should be designed to put still more strain on the existing buyer/supplier relationship.

Super-Specific Needs Appraisal Questions

Aim: *Determine sales potential and buying cycle.*
Q: "How much and how often do you buy?"

Aim: *Why are prospective buyers talking to you?*
Q: "What sort of problems have you been having?"

Aim: *Indication of accustomed quality and price range.*
Q: "What company or product/service are you using *now*?"

Aim: *Discover long-term account potential.*
Q: "What are you looking for? What are the company's goals?"

Aim: *Find out if this is a sale for today, next month, next year.*

Q: "When do you need a quote? When will the order be placed? When do you need the product/service?"

Aim: *Find new markets.*
Q: "Who is the end-user? how/where will the product/service be used?"

Aim: *Locate the decision-maker.*
Q: "Who else do we (not 'I') need to talk to? Who else affects the buying decision?"

Aim: *Establish the contact's buying authority.*
Q: "What is your exact responsibility for this project?"

Aim: *Discover the level of service from the present vendor.*
Q: "How long has it been taking to get a quote/delivery/*after-sales service*?"

Aim: *Uncover more potential problems with the current supplier.*
Q: "How do you think you could do better? What other problems have you been having? What are you trying for, but can't seem to achieve?"

Aim: *Mention product/service benefits.*
Q: "What do you know about my company/services/products?"

Aim: *Find out their required quality and price.*
Q: "What sort of quality is important? How crucial is price? What's your price-*range* or budget for this purchase?"

Aim: *Expand your market.*
Q: "Who do you know here, or at branches or subsidiaries, who could use this product?"

Aim: *Establish the price-sensitivity of your product/ service.*
Q: "What percentage of your finished product consists of my product? (High percentage = high price-sensitivity and vice versa.)

Aim: *Final check that nothing has been missed.*
Q: What else do you look for in a top-rate supplier?

These are all "open-ended" questions, using the journalistic Who, What, Why, Where, How, and When, which reflexively demand more than just those minimum "yes" or "no" answers. In one form or another, they apply to every industry or profession, but to make the most of them, you must expand on the examples, and tailor them according to your verbal style and needs and what it is you're selling.

Write down the answers to all of your Appraisal questions as you receive them, not only to build a visual framework for the sale, but to show prospects that you consider them important and that you place a high value on their responses. Draw attention to this with, "Could you repeat that, please? I want to be sure to get your answer down correctly."

Some old pros laugh at the idea of asking Needs Appraisal questions, believing that their knowledge of their industry means that they already know what their customers need. True, they do know most of the answers before asking the questions, but this doesn't lessen the importance of a thorough Appraisal session with every new prospect. These old pros are focussing on themselves, and missing the whole point of the exercise, which is to instill confidence in the customer via the asking of questions that reveal the sales person as having a very high level of knowledge and expertise in the field.

Tactical and Strategic Listening

The Appraisal emphasizes asking the right questions, but it also includes the need to listen and comprehend—skills that receive much lip service but less real attention than they deserve.

Tactical listening, as practiced by so many sales people, describes short-term information gathering from a narrow, front-line viewpoint, with the goal of an immediate sale. Strategic listening, on the other hand, looks down the road at the long-term prosperity and potential of an account, and perfectly illustrates the small but vitally important incremental differences in attitude and technique separating sales plodders from star performers.

Because no single sale exists in a vacuum unrelated to the complete sales picture, every call should include both types of listening. This means that a truly professional seller learns to listen on two quite different levels at the same time. By asking carefully designed Needs Appraisal questions relating to today's sale, she is able to manage the Tactical listening session, while remaining on the alert for those less-obvious Strategic responses.

Strategic listening differs from Tactical, not only in its long-term, big-picture aspects, but also in demanding a peripheral sensitivity for *spoken* answers to *unspoken* questions. Without realizing it, prospects and

Tactical and Strategic Listening

> **TACTICAL**
> - Short Term / Narrow Focus
> - Immediate Sale
> - Predictable Responses

> **STRATEGIC**
> - Long Term / Wide Ranging
> - Unpredictable Responses
> - Unspoken Questions
> - Spoken Answers

customers alike use these "soft" responses to acknowledge and reward our genuine interest in them and their problems, and to satisfy a pressing need to feel important and recognized.

An accomplished West Coast salesman says his relationship with a big auto parts supplier is a good example of Tactical and Strategic listening. He has taken the time to develop a warm personal relationship with the Purchasing Agent, and now spends most of a day calling on this account.

The morning is reserved for paperwork and Tactical listening, but at exactly noon, instead of going to lunch, they always begin a long tour of a huge warehouse that is the nerve-center of the business. This ritual never varies, and invariably includes a description of the coup involved in purchasing every item in every bin. Even with all those hours on concrete floors, the salesman never complains, for this is Strategic listening time.

Not being a psychologist, it took him months to see that the Purchasing Agent, starved of recognition by a domineering president, is only truly happy in the warehouse, where he can see the results of his hard work. He literally *has* to show his companion what a great job he is doing, even to revealing his sources, costs, stock levels, and order destinations.

Later, the salesman searches his memory for details of all he has heard. Tacical listening has helped him build a million dollar account. Strategic listening and enormous patience have given him access to invaluable production-planning and marketing information not available to other reps who are too busy rushing to their next call to take the time to listen Strategically.

Everything You Need to Know

The generation of sales people that grew up in the 1960s has been described as one that watches rather than listens, and enjoys seeing life's problems solved within the thirty to sixty minute span of a TV show.

But career selling demands that you take enough interest in what other people are saying to listen without interrupting, sometimes for hours at a time.

The truth of this statement is substantiated by the experience of a Midwestern regional manager for a big Chicago company that wanted to buy out one of her key accounts. Stifling her serious misgivings, she followed instructions to ask the customer company's president several questions, such as what his total sales were, what percentage of this was domestic and what export, and how much inventory he carried. As she had expected, he flew into a fury at her effrontery, and shouted that his was a private corporation and that he didn't have to give this information to anyone, least of all her! In fact, it was only her long-standing business and social relationship with this man's family that saved the account for her.

The dust had settled by the time of her next visit, and there was no mention of his previous explosion during their as-usual pleasant meeting. It was only as she was leaving that she suddenly realized that the president, seemingly without being aware of it himself, had given her oblique answers to two of the forbidden questions.

Two meetings later, having been alerted to listen with great care, she had all the asked-for information in one form or another, and was able to send a "mission-completed" report to her company. Clear proof that, in sales, if you listen long enough, you will learn all you need to know.

Time to Take Charge

The saying "The easiest people to sell are sales people" comes true when customers "sell" *us* on the idea of *their* managing the sales consultation. From then on, we endure uneasy sensations of being swept along on their strong wills, of being merely passengers who have lost all control of events. But, fortunately for us, recognizable opportunities for reasserting our authority arise throughout the sale, and even right into the Close.

Just such a "take charge" opportunity occurs at the start of the Appraisal. While prospects are still responding to Rapport-building questions and comments, they are also subconsciously waiting for your signal that it is time to get down to business. And you can give this signal simply by sitting up straight in your chair, by deliberately letting the conversation flag, or by taking out a pen and pad and laying them in front of you.

Without being abrupt about it, blend your first Appraisal question into the conversation, and write down the answer. This harmonizing of social and business queries enables you to glide smoothly into the listing of priorities that will be the focus of the next stage—Demonstration.

Suspects Who Aren't Prospects

Habit will always be a sales person's greatest enemy, just as time is our most valuable commodity, and the first priority is always to find out if you are dealing with a genuine prospect who is worth a serious time-investment, or with a "suspect" who is just wasting your time. Using the Super-Specific Needs Appraisal Questions, five to ten minutes should be long enough to determine if you are talking to a "live" one or not.

But for pros there are no wasted calls, and calls to apparently worthless "suspects" are no exception. Thank them for their time, and then ask for referrals to subsidiaries or other divisions, or even their old company, which perhaps can use your services and products. Research shows that buyers rate very highly sales people who help them with alternative sources for products they are unable to supply. Tell them where they can find what they need, and you leave behind friends who will recommend you and look for ways to buy from you in the future.

Second Person Singular

As you question to Appraise needs, mirror body language (the 25 percent response), and provide the reassurance and approbation that lessen tension, take care to observe the personality of the person opposite you. Of the dominant personality types, this prospect will be: a Toiler, a Mover, a Gossip, a Director, or a combination of one or more of these types.

PERSONALITY	CHARACTERISTICS
Toiler	Systematic, Low-key, Amiable, Tolerant, Punctual, Unexcitable, Fatalistic, Painstaking, Deliberate, Reserved, Collector.
Mover	Hurried, Outspoken, Ascendant, Issue-oriented, Passionate, Achiever, Order-giver, Quick-acting, Status-seeker.
Gossip	Likes people, Time-waster, Attractive, Verbal wanderer, Sympathetic, Out-going, Lively, Emotional, Enthusiastic.
Director	Introvert, Good manager, Appraiser, Organizer, Remote, Factual, Down-to-earth, Judgmental, Decisive, Detached.

Accommodating yourself, in words and actions, to their dominant personality characteristics certainly seems to make the people in question easier to sell, particularly when the seller also knows his or her own type of personality.

Even a limited amount of self-knowledge enables one to anticipate and avoid potential clashes of temperament.

But in the long run, your own obvious integrity and genuine desire to help will always carry more weight in founding lasting and profitable relationships than worrying too much about prospects' personalities.

Solid Gold Leads

The group of students arguing during a break in sales training were obviously confused. Having heard so much about "referrals" being the easiest sales to make, they didn't understand why they were Closing such a low percentage of these "solid gold" leads. And as we talked, still more students gathered round to agree that selling referrals was a problem for them as well.

In looking for answers, we divided the leads into two categories: "A" (Active) prospects, who initiate contact following the recommendation of a satisfied customer, and "P" (Passive) ones, who are contacted by suppliers at the suggestion of a satisfied customer.

"A" leads obviously have the higher priority, but in either case, the seller has reached a highly qualified prospect with an assumed need, and an easy sale should result. But an informal survey of these students found that, on the contrary, for most of them, about 50 percent of Active and 70 percent of Passive referrals did not turn into sales.

The key to this puzzle was found to lie in the word "assumed." Apparently, for these sales people, the idea that a pleased third party had highly recommended their service or product had translated itself into the idea of an automatic sale. In their minds, the necessary social and emotional Links had already been made, leading them to believe that they already knew such prospects well enough to eliminate the need to Link, establish Rapport, or Appraise.

By assuming that a referral lead was already almost sold, they neglected the first half of the sale and threw the baby out with the bath water. In effect, by taking these top-qualified prospects for granted, they very often even managed to completely change the prospects' minds about buying from a previously favored source!

By a coincidence, shortly after this discussion, my company signed a consulting contract with a Manhattan firm whose Closing rate for both "A" and "P" leads was even lower than the percentages those students had projected. Starting with the expectation of a guaranteed order, this firm's sales force assumed an unwarranted knowledge of prospects' requirements, tended to ignore the logical progression of the sale, and moved hurriedly into the Close. They pushed too hard, dispensed too much unwanted information, and kept on "assuming" as the sale slipped away from them.

Having lost the chance to construct a proper sales framework, when things went wrong they could only rush forward, like someone trying desperately to escape a quicksand, in the vain hope of correcting the mess poor selling had created.

First, we asked them to treat all referral leads as "super cold" calls, requiring even more than the full treatment. We even termed such leads "451's" (after Ray Bradbury's *Fahrenheit 451*), and instructed the sales force to take extra care with the initial three stages of all referral sales. To increase prospects' comfort-levels, the Link would always include allusions to satisfied customers who gave the original referrals. Example: "By the way, your name came up when I saw Jim Smith yesterday, and he asked me to say 'Hello.' "

By making these important changes in their Approach to referrals, the reps not only increased sales to this class of prospect, but generated a high rate of further referred leads, to perpetuate the success cycle.

Anyone who gives referred prospects this extra attention will soon find that they do indeed become solid gold leads, and their easiest sales.

Time and the Seller

In selling, as in every other human activity, there's "time" and there's "timing," and of the two, concentrate on the latter, because a highly developed sense of timing is one of the great building blocks of successful selling.

Perfect sales timing, born of intuition, is incredibly valuable to those lucky enough to possess it, but when it is so intuitive, so hard to catalogue, it must always be hidden from sales managers who insist on ordering every move according to a strict timetable. And such are the pressures on today's sales people, from competition and computerized "tickle" files, that only the strongest-willed manage to preserve their right to listen first to their sense of timing as they sell.

For me, timing has long been an internal clock that tells me almost unerringly when to make a personal call, when to follow up by phone, and when to check on an order. It is the ultimate expression of the old sales admonition, "Work smart, not hard," and is a tremendous time-saver.

The test of timing is when customers consistently tell you that you must have ESP because they were just going to call for your assistance or to place an order. Obedience to this intuition hones, refines, and makes it more powerful; denying it in favor of another's instructions causes it to become unreliable, and eventually to wither away.

Timing is defined as the "art of regulating the speed of performance . . . to ensure maximum effectiveness . . . ," so think twice before allowing your perception of perfect timing to be overruled by anyone.

Tough Guys and the Guilt Factor

Don Jacobs, a man who consistently sets standards for integrity and achievement as Sales Manager of Fel-Pro's Industrial Division, always had the same reply when I complained about a customer: "If you can sell the tough guys you can sell anyone!" What he meant by this remark was that customers who, for reasons of stubborness or extreme loyalty to a long-time supplier, are tough to sell will present exactly the same difficulties to someone else following you into the account. Sell the tough guys, and you build behind you an almost impregnable wall against the competition.

Looking at "impossible" prospects from this point of view makes it easier to recover from whole strings of cancelled appointments, from rudeness and indifference, and to come out punching once again. So many reps just dread calling on these people, who employ biting sarcasm as a negotiating tool, laugh at them behind their backs, walk out of meetings without explanation, and have been buying from the same supplier for twenty years. They treat all sales people the same way (with the exception of their favored vendor). Their information on your type of product is probably years out of date; they don't care that they pay too much. But if you *can* sell them, they'll be loyal to you for a long time.

Take the case of an Indiana rubber manufacturer's salesman calling on Western States Highway Departments to seek their engineers' approval of a new bridge-deck expansion joint system. At one particular bridge design "section," he dropped in to meet a newly arrived design engineer. Crossing a large office to give the engineer a product engineering manual, he should have noticed from the man's fixed expression that something was wrong. The engineer ignored his greeting to grab the binder and fling it across the room, so that it burst open in the doorway. As he did so, he shouted, "I'm not going to approve this 'rubbish,' so get it and yourself out of here!"

Forcing himself to remain silent, the rep, on his knees, took his time carefully reassembling the manual, and then stood up to say quietly, "I'm very sorry that you feel like that, I'll come back in four weeks." He literally had nightmares about their next meeting, and when the day arrived, delayed the inevitable by first seeing every other contact in the building—and in the eyes of all of them, imagined that he could read sympathy for his forthcoming ordeal.

Walking through the same doorway that had witnessed his embarrassment a month earlier, and braced for another confrontation, he was stunned at the difference in his reception. Smiling, and with hand outstretched, his prospect came out from behind his desk with inquiries about his health, and profuse apologies for his earlier behavior.

Still smarting from the worst experience of his career, the salesman brushed aside the engineer's excuses about problems at home and at work, and stuck closely to business. For his part, the engineer interpreted this as an unwillingness to forgive and forget, and redoubled his efforts to atone for what had happened. So complete was the role-reversal, in fact, that the salesman was at a loss to know how to handle it. Eventually, things settled down, and the engineer not only approved the complete expansion joint system outright, but became its staunch supporter for all but the largest bridges.

Furthermore, as long as he continued to call on him, the rep never completely let the engineer off the hook. Every now and then, he'd give his conscience a little jab, and the engineer would start apologizing all over again. Soon after that, the expansion joint would be "sole-spec'd" for yet another big project.*

The salesman said afterwards that this incident taught him always to stay above his customers' tantrums, and to stifle the temptation to argue—because sooner or later, they'll not only feel guilty, but will be impelled by this guilt to make it up to you.

Winning Actions and Attitudes

- **Third Pillar Affirmations will support you in the Appraisal.**
- **Ask yourself, "What exactly is it that I'm selling?"**
- **Personalize your own Specific Questions.**
- **Sell the CONCEPT.**
- **Ask, "What are they buying?"**
- **Listen Tactically and Strategically.**
- **Study that "Second Person Singular."**
- **Take care with referrals.**
- **Develop perfect sales timing.**
- **Sell tough guys by using the guilt factor.**

*A "sole specification" is usually written around the product specifications of a single manufacturer, with the aim of excluding inferior competing products, or forcing their manufacturers to meet superior specs (if they can do so without patent infringement). For a sales person, a "sole spec" is the Holy Grail!

THE FOURTH PILLAR/ THE FOURTH STEP DEMONSTRATE

Definition: Illustrate, Display, Exhibit, Show Undeniable Evidence.

Key Affirmation: "My willingness to *learn* causes ideas of prosperity to flow to me, and through me to my customers!"

Approximate Length of Step: 10 to 30 minutes.

Key Actions: Present 60 percent/Listen 40 percent.

Key Attitudes: Help prospects to see how your product or service meets their *expressed* needs and to encourage their active participation in all aspects of your *demonstration*.

One Word Worth a Thousand Pictures

English people in the United States soon get used to being referred to as "Limeys," and to being ribbed for favoring an odd-sounding broad "a" in words such as "after" and "bathroom." They either laugh it off, ignore it, or work that British usage for all it's worth. But sometimes it takes a real-life experience to gauge the effect of a particular way of speaking on others.

As regional sales manager for a big industrial chemicals company, it was part of my job to train distributors, manufacturer's reps, and direct sales people to sell metal-filled, plant-maintenance epoxies to paper mills, factories, and shipyards in the Western United States and Western Canada.

Instead of our steel, stainless-steel, or bronze epoxies, we always demonstrated the bright, shiny, aluminium ones. And invariably, as the compound was mixed and formed into metal parts, or to accept threaded fittings, there would be accompanying derisive comments and sniggers from the audience, at the Limey salesman who couldn't say "aluminum." And the leg-pulling would continue, days or weeks later, when we worked with the same crews on maintenance problems in the field. So, in case you were wondering, the extra "i" in aluminium, or in speciality (in the story about the steel sales woman), is not there to be pedantic or pompous, but because it's *memorable*. A small thing, perhaps, but years later, on returning to one of those British Columbian mills, a big maintenance foreman stopped as we approached each other, looked me up and down, and exclaimed, "I know you, you're the guy who says 'ALUMINIUM'!"

Our products worked as advertised, no better and no worse than the competition's, but the unfamiliar sound of that one word stuck in the memories of those maintenance people, causing them to think of us first when they needed industrial chemicals. So strong was this association that the successful sales of a whole line of my firm's products within my huge region hinged on this simple Demonstration of aluminium epoxy.

So try to be memorable when you sell, and particularly when you Demonstrate. Not ludicrous, *memorable*!

Calls + Demos = Sales

A popular sign hanging in many sales offices features the above equation, but this only tells half the story, as it says nothing about the *quality* of the Demonstration, nor of the customer's vital role in it.

Winning Demonstrations make clear-cut demands on sales people, as follows:

- The "Demo" should relate directly to a written framework of prospects' expressed needs and wants, resulting from a careful Appraisal.
- The "Demo" must be "visual," brief, easy to duplicate, and always controlled.
- It should address prospects' primary buying preoccupations, largely ignoring minor concerns.
- An accompanying "advisory" selling style will assure prospects of the sales person's genuine interest in helping them make the right buying decision.

The Magic Touch: Customer Involvement

The more you are able to direct customers in touching, smelling, looking at, listening to, or tasting what is being Demonstrated, the more control you have of the sale, and the more emotionally engaged they become, as they begin to identify with the product and to sell themselves. This is why all Demos should be simple enough for prospects to understand and perform themselves without difficulty.

Tangibles v. Intangibles——
Immediate v. Delayed Results

Generally, tangible products are easier to Demonstrate than intangible concepts or services, and this is also true of services or products that show immediate, rather than delayed, results. If you are lucky enough to sell "instant" adhesives, your Demonstration may consist of only a few drops of glue, two pieces of rubber, and ten seconds to Demonstrate a dramatic three-thousand pound bond. But while it is often considered more difficult to sell intangible "concepts" than solid "nuts and bolts" products, these same intangibles do have their own clear sales advantages.

- Intangibles are never "out of stock" or unobtainable due to production problems.
- They are not only always "on the shelf" and readily available but can be adapted in moments to fit almost any special requirements, in ways not possible with tangible items.
- Demonstrations of tangibles are limited to "what you see is what you get." The brochures, articles, and testimonials used in intangibles Demonstrations offer skilled sales communicators limitless opportunities to involve prospects' imaginations in the vivid verbal "benefits pictures" they paint. As they do so, they move the sale rapidly forward.

It's My Baby

Sales people who are not personally involved with product design, engineering, and manufacture find it easy to remain calm, objective, and sales-focussed even in the face of harsh criticism of their company's products. But "creative" people—designers, artists, writers, inventors—are closely involved with every stage of their product's development. The intensity of this association causes them to hate selling, and especially Demonstrating, and they are seriously hurt by prospects' criticisms and indifference to their "baby." This very natural hypersensitivity makes for bad selling, hinders careers, and leaves these people at the mercy of experienced buyers.

For instance, graphic designers will meekly follow an art director's instructions to "dump your samples on the old light box, or on my desk . . . ," then writhe with frustration as the hard-boiled prospect flips casually through years of work with barely a glance, and in thirty seconds flat. And before they realize what is happening, they've gathered up their samples again and stumbled from the room, saleless and desperate.

Get Out of the Sales Rut

Because their industry's selling "norm" is to Demonstrate and try to Close the sale on the first encounter, they do just what everyone else does, even if this means repeatedly banging their heads against a wall.

They could so easily avoid the ego battering, rejection, and depression by breaking the mold, and just going in with a pencil and pad. Wouldn't the art director throw them out? Not if they started by explaining that they always treat the first call as an introductory and fact-finding mission, to save prospects' time by finding out how they can best serve their interests.

By leaving their Achilles' heel, their precious work, at home, they are automatically less sensitive, defensive, and argumentative (all sale killers), and can quietly guide the meeting, while evaluating the prospect and Appraising his needs. As soon as common ground has been identified, a follow-up "Demonstration and Closing" meeting is easily arranged. Leaving their samples behind not only relieves these sales people of the burden of having to sell every unqualified "suspect" they meet, but encourages them to concentrate their sales time on a short list of highly-qualified prospective customers.

A Generation Without Service

The best Demonstrations are not confined to product displays and customer involvement, but also include active discussion of the follow-up support and service to be provided as part of a written or assumed agreement. Unfortunately, two generations of Americans have grown up without ever experiencing real service. They may pay endless lip service to the concept, but most are unable or unwilling to provide it to others.

Service used to mean products of the highest quality, manufactured, supplied, and supported with constant attention to the desires of customers, who, unlike ourselves, didn't have to check every purchase to make sure it wasn't flawed. They could generally assume that much time, pride, and care had been devoted to bringing the finest materials to as near a perfect finished product as possible. Craftsmen served long apprenticeships to refine their skills, plastic was in its infancy, and the "planned obsolescence" swindle had not yet been widely perpetrated on a complacent public.

After the Second World War, the old aristocratic market, which demanded perfection at reasonable prices, was elbowed aside by a gullible, undemanding, and often frightened mass market. This made goods and services available to millions of people who previously had no access to them. But it has condemned the concept of true service to at least temporary oblivion. The old system has been replaced by a climate of "false-service." A very high concept has been reduced, via misleading advertising and unkept promises, to no more than an overworked seven-letter word.

As front-line sales people, we are the keepers of the flame of true service, and must do whatever we can to guard and renew it. Service, with a capital S, is not complicated; it just means telling customers the exact truth of what they can expect in product quality and support from your company, and then moving Heaven and Earth to make sure those promises are met. If sales people everywhere performed to the highest attainable standards, every time they sold, while demanding Service themselves every time they bought, the universal serviceless blight of "communerism" would quickly recede, and we would all enjoy true Service again.

Selling Your Value Package

By carefully handing samples, brochures, drawings, or photographs to prospects in order to emphasize their value, you can further extend your control of this aspect of the sale. To stimulate customer interest in the Demonstration process, use such open-ended questions as: "What's your reaction to this feature . . . ?" or "Tell me what you think about our approach to solving that problem . . . ?" People are usually reassured by the sound of their own voices and will readily give their judgments, impressions, thoughts, observations, and criticisms of your product or service.

In this way, they not only become their own powerful advocates for the things you sell, they give you the benefit of their product/service improvement ideas. Regularly practiced, this way of selling yields invaluable product and market research to keep you ahead of competitors, while indirectly lowering your company's design, production, and sales costs.

But in your eagerness to talk about features, never forget that the primary buying impulses—Gain, Vanity, Enjoyment, and Tranquility—reflect the fact that most people buy emotionally from benefits, rather than logically from features. That sales people who know this still only sell features indicates either that they don't understand the true differences between the two, or that they don't know how to use customers' concerns to decide which are the best features and benefits for use in a Demonstration. This weakness seriously affects their sales success because the very core of what they sell—their Value Package—depends on the interrelationships among these Concerns, Features, and Benefits.

Concerns: Disturb, trouble, make anxious, or engage the interest.

Features: Are marks, characteristics, elements, components, or aspects.

Benefits: Are advantages, favors, profits, boons,

gains, services, kindnesses, gifts, bless-
ings, prosperity. Our word *benefit* is derived from the French *bien fait*—do good.

Building a Value Package

The selling of Value Packages is both easy and effective, as they add substance and focus to "concept" selling, discussed earlier. But before it can be sold, a Package
must be constructed from the following sales constit-
uents:

- Customers' dominant concerns, coupled with
  the weaknesses of their competitors.
- Product or service features that address those
  concerns, and highlight those weaknesses.
- Benefits, derived from the features, that satisfy
  customers, further magnify competitors' problems, and reinforce your own company's over-
  all strengths.

Even if you know your customers, your products,
your industry, and your competition very well, building a Value Package is not a "one-shot" project but a
continuous process of upgrading and review in antic-
ipation of market changes.

The actual, edited Value Package that follows will
illustrate these points, and spark ideas on how to put
together your own personalized version.

Example of a Value Package

Company: Tri-State Binders, Inc. (fictitious name)
Products: Custom vinyl ring-binders; audio, video and computer software packaging; and custom leather office products.
Goal: Increase sales by encouraging sales people to sell the many clear-cut advantages of Tri-State products, instead of just talking about binders.

Concerns/Features/Benefits

Customer Concerns and the Features and Benefits that Address Them

Concern: Entrusting important projects to remote, careless, high-volume producers, or to small, ill-equipped, under-financed "job shops."
Feature: Large, modern, well-equipped, centrally-located main plant.
Benefits: High quality, state of-the-art production. Accessible, customer-oriented staff. Reasonably-priced "local" deliveries.

Concern: Rigid, unresponsive, automated production methods.
Feature: Up-to-date, "custom" plant—with well-trained, rural work force.
Benefits: Quick response to complex, short-run orders. Compensates for late ordering and end-user planning problems. Makes buyer look good.

Concern: Uneven quality "buy outs," and unreliable foreign products.

Feature: Main plant makes virtually 100 percent of products sold.

Benefits: Customers enjoy consistent quality control and personal attention to detail. Reliable "short haul" deliveries v. delayed imports. Production flexibility, to handle the most difficult orders.

Concern: Heavy costs of storing large binder orders in limited-space, high-rent office locations.

Feature: Very large finished product storage area in plant.

Benefits: Immediate cost and space savings for customers, who can order production runs for storage at plant, for later just-in-time staged deliveries.

Concern: Having to buy from several suppliers of loose leaf products to meet a variety of product needs.

Feature: Full line of binder-related products and services.

Benefits: "One-stop shopping" allows buyer to save time and money by dealing with one sales person, one vendor company, just one purchase order, etc. Consolidation of shipments results in considerable freight costs savings.

Concern: On the part of big corporations, when they have to buy from small binder-manufacturers, which may be under-financed, poorly managed, and slow to respond.

Feature: Old, well-established, financially sound company, with many Fortune 500 clients.

Benefits: Peace of mind. "Corporate" approach to business. Reliable supplier that is here to stay.

Concern: Frequent binder price increases and inconsistent materials availability.

Feature: 180,000-square-foot plant. Well-financed company.

Benefits: Stable, competitive prices. Cost savings and consistently available materials, resulting from ability to buy and stock mill-runs of vinyl and carloads of metals.

Concern: Inability to contact sales person quickly, to get rush quotes, or to check on status of orders in house.

Feature: Large, strategically positioned sales force, a sales coordination department, and "quick quotes" system.

Benefits: No customer in Tri-State's marketing area is ever more than 45 minutes from a sales person. "Quick quotes" service generally allows same-day pricing, compared with competitors taking up to six days. Sales coordinators provide peace of mind by tracking all orders through the plant to supply current production status or delivery times.

Concern: Occasional competitive price-cutting and attendant poor quality materials and finish.

Feature: Unlike the competition, Tri-State's concentration is on value and length of product service, not just on price.

Benefits: Highest quality materials, including heavier gauge virgin vinyl, and metals. Provision of design assistance to achieve longer product life for customers.

Concern: By Manhattan customers, for ultra-fast order turnaround.
Feature: New York City small-order plant.
Benefits: Immediate response to city customers' rush order requirements. Local pick-up and delivery. Five-day completion cycle.

Total the Benefits

It is the sum of the benefits drawn from a list of concerns and features that makes up the Value Package, and it is this benefits Value Package that you sell. The best Value Packages are never cast in concrete—they are always either getting better or going out of date as markets change and competition fluctuates. So it is definitely in your interest to keep on updating and improving your Value Package, with new features and greater benefits. Don't relax your efforts until it is as good as it can be, because this Value Package is literally your fame and fortune—it's what you sell!

Value-to-Cost Ratio

Speaking honestly, a large percentage of American sales people would admit that they consider the services and products they sell as being worth much less than what they ask for them.

They approach selling with the attitude, "I'll be lucky to get an order today." And guess what. With this mindset, they are extremely fortunate to sell anything at all!

Or they see product value as barely equal to cost—still a hard sell.

The remaining few, who make most of the sales, *know*, from the benefits they offer, that their products are worth far more than the selling price.

This striking difference in attitudes means that members of the last group, going out to present such high value at such low cost, not only confidently expect to sell, they consistently write orders!

Their conviction of exceptional value offered not only enables them to get their price but helps them to make far better livings for themselves, and higher profits for their companies. This means that firms struggling in a highly competitive market can often actually raise

Selling a Value Package

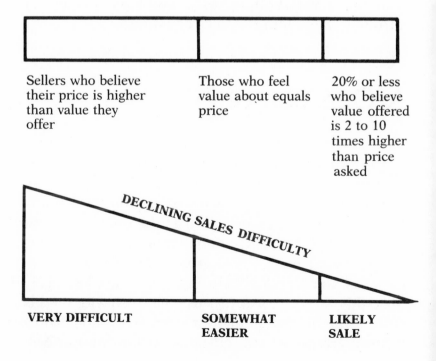

| Sellers who believe their price is higher than value they offer | Those who feel value about equals price | 20% or less who believe value offered is 2 to 10 times higher than price asked |

DECLINING SALES DIFFICULTY

| VERY DIFFICULT | SOMEWHAT EASIER | LIKELY SALE |

both prices and profits as a result of employing ethical, value-oriented selling.

The confidence and enjoyment of selling value give a small percentage of sales people an invincible edge over competitors selling only on price. Price-selling is, after all, only an endless, demeaning competition to see who can go the lowest. It also virtually guarantees poor pay and low profits.

Just as price-selling drags sellers into a bottomless vortex of devalued products, value-selling constantly opens for its practitioners new and wider vistas of opportunity, success, and profitability. Value-selling knows no ceilings, no limits!

Undeniably, there are "price" industries, where the only questions one ever seems to hear are "How much is it?" or "What's the cost?" And yet, even here, some sales people are outstandingly successful because they firmly believe that their customers really want more than just a rock-bottom price, and they manage to introduce value into the sales equation.

A Question of Price

The perfect time to raise the subject of price is after you've established prospects' needs and Demonstrated a superior capacity to satisfy them. But perhaps because they have so often been sold only on price, many customers behave as though it is the only thing that matters, and try to force anticipatory price questions on the sales person from early in the meeting. (Customers who are well-sold from the start are less likely to do this, so you can always use their behavior on this point as an indication of your sales professionalism.)

Always respond to the question "What's your price?"

with a relaxed smile and demeanor and a welcoming remark, such as "I'm glad you mentioned that . . ." or "Price is always important, but before getting into details, let me ask you one more question . . ." Or, "The value of our service (or the performance of this product) is directly related to price, so you'll want the various cost/value options that we offer . . ." Or, "Do you have an approximate budget in mind for this project?"

Introducing the Price

Introducing the price is not difficult when sellers first take a moment to: 1) focus on the positive value to cost ratio they offer; 2) make sure there are no distractions; 3) look steadily at the prospect; 4) state the price; 5) keep quiet. When supported by facts on expected savings, comparative costs, and measurable bottom line results, a firm belief in value-offered will be transmitted to the other person, and make him or her more likely to accept the price without argument.

"Your Price Is Too High!"

For sales people, no words in selling carry the sheer fear and intimidation that this dread phrase does. They don't know how to counter it, nor realize that it is often designed to soften them up. It is the world's oldest buyer's "con," a merciless probe for a better price. The best responses are usually relaxed, smiling, open-ended questions or comments, designed to create opportunities for yourself to re-present the price-justifying value points of a product or service as you welcome the toughest objections. Here are some very good examples of "circular" objection-responses that not only reduce any remaining tension or resentment in the buyer, but also create perfect opportunities for you to restate one or more of the benefits in your package.

Prospect: *"Your price is too high!"*
Sales: "What makes you say that?"
Prospect: (Mentions lower quotes from competitors.)
Sales: (Smiles, nods agreement, restates buyer's key wants and needs, shows how value points meet needs and justify cost.)

Prospect: *"Your price is too high!"*
Sales: "I'm sure you have good reasons for saying that?"
Prospect: (Gives reasons.)
Sales: (Same final response as in the preceding example.)

Prospect: *"Your price is too high!"*
Sales: "I understand your concern for price, but have you taken into account . . .?" (Moves directly into values restatement and cost-justification.)

Prospect: *"Your price is too high!"*
Sales: "I'm disappointed when you say that, because it means I did a poor job of explaining the special values contained in our offer . . ." (Pauses for prospect's reply, or moves into restatement and justification.)

The Price-Cut Vortex

Whatever the pressures to get the order, *never* give a firm price and then cut it without receiving an appropriate quid pro quo. To do so would be to surrender all your new-found professionalism, and jump right into the bottomless price-selling vortex with everyone else.

There are valid reasons for lowering price, which vary to some extent from industry to industry. They include:

- Customer increases size of order.
- Instead of demanding shipments to several locations, customer agrees to take complete shipment at one address, and handle drop-shipments from there.
- Customer signs "blanket" purchase order for larger purchases over longer periods than originally discussed.
- Discount takes the form of an advertising allowance.
- Customer agrees to stock and distribute your line.

Winning Actions and Attitudes

- **Declare the Fourth Pillar Affirmations forcefully every day for one week.**
- **Be memorable when you Demonstrate.**
- **Constantly reassure and involve customers, and**

check on your progress by probing for their ideas, opinions, suggestions, and impressions.
- Control the Demonstration.
- Keep the flame of true Service.
- Ethical, value-based selling.
- Relaxed, welcoming, open-ended questions and comments, to counter objections and create opportunity for value points restatement.

THE FIFTH PILLAR/ THE FIFTH STEP VERIFY

Definition: Authenticate, Establish, Corroborate, Substantiate, Confirm Truth of—from the Latin *verificare*, to make true.
Key Affirmation: "I have full *authority* to control my sales success, and every aspect of my selling career!"
Approximate Length of Step: 5 to 15 minutes.
Key Actions: Explain 50 percent/Listen 50 percent.
Key Attitudes: Customers are entitled to clear proof that what we tell them is true.

Never Trust a Stranger

Prospects are only human, and they are far more likely to believe what other people say about you, your company, and its products or services, than they are to believe what you yourself say. In short, they expect you to provide clear proof of what you've Demonstrated before trusting you and allowing a buying relationship to develop.

References are recognized as necessary to "close the sale" on a job. A new plane won't sell without an airworthiness certificate. Positive thermo-luminescence tests must accompany rare ceramic objects if they are to realize their full value at auction. And yet, many sales people completely ignore this need to satisfy customers' very human desire for proof.

Photographs, articles, books, audio and video tapes, independent reports, and graphs and statistics all constitute excellent sales Verification material and can easily be generated or assembled by you or your company. There are also testimonial letters (which often make the best Verifiers), but here we have to rely on satisfied customers to provide them.

The Art of Getting the Testimonial

You will need testimonial letters for all types of selling situations, so get into the habit of asking for them every time your company delivers exceptional quality or service. Call your customer while the project is still "hot," to say how happy you are that they are pleased, and how much it would help you if they would write you a recommendation. However, because clients tend to write unsuitable, or even weird, testimonials when left to their own devices, it is up to you to guide their hands. Either suggest a range of topics—quality, increased profits, personal attention, creativity, fast turnaround, or others of concerns to your industry—to be covered in the letter, or, better still, write the letter yourself.

Write four or five modular and interchangeable paragraphs that can be easily altered for future reuse —one topic per paragraph, and not more than a one-page letter. Deliver it personally to your customer. Don't mail it or entrust it to a secretary, but make sure to hand it directly to the person concerned. Explain this action by remarking that because everyone has too much to read, and too many letters to write these days, you have taken the liberty of writing the letter yourself.

And stress that you don't want the person to sign anything that isn't 100 percent true.

Without exception, each time I have used this method, the customer has been grateful for my thoughtfulness, has briefly scanned what I have written, and has handed it to a secretary for typing on company letterhead. And I have left with exactly the testimonial I needed. Incidentally, no dates or datable events should be referred to in the body of the letter, as these can reduce its useful life from several years to a few months. For the same reason, dates are often omitted from the tops of testimonial letters as well.

Reproducing Testimonials

Instead of photocopying testimonials, which cheapens their appearance and reduces their impact on prospects, have them run-off by your local quick-printer. For a small premium over the cost of photocopies, he can match the letter's paper stock and the Pantone Matching System (PMS) color of the logo, to turn out a reproduction that is almost indistinguishable from the original. These "printed" testimonials impress prospects, add welcome color to a presentation, and strengthen the Verification step. They are also useful in assembling matching testimonial sets for larger sales forces. Better presentation quality for articles, reports, and statistics can be achieved by photocopying onto higher-quality, off-white, or colored paper.

The Testimonial Culture

Some industries make constant use of testimonials in selling; others hardly use them at all. Some companies use testimonials only in their advertising, and call them "case histories"; others introduce them as an active part of their face-to-face selling as well. This lack of a constant in the use of testimonials suggests that there is within each industry a predilection for their use or relative non-use, and raises the question of which services and products benefit most from third-party-testimonial selling. This is a question that can only be answered by individual entrepreneurs and sales people.

Even when testimonials are not used with much genuine vigor, the practice of requiring members of a sales force to obtain them from their customers will garner invaluable marketing information and hard evidence of exactly how these customers perceive a supplier and its products.

Asking customers for testimonials stimulates them to focus on the things that make you a valuable supplier, and this in turn can result in a surge of appreciative orders and referral business.

Reinforce, Reassure, Ratify

At this stage in the sale, buyers' earlier fears of what you are trying to do to them, and of what can happen to them if they make a mistake in buying from you, frequently resurface to derail the sale, and it is time to reinforce, reassure, and ratify to calm those fears.

Reinforce their confidence in the high worth and problem-solving capability of your offering by reiterating the Value Package benefits, with Verification that has been adapted to their most pressing needs and concerns.

Reassure them that their personal and business interests are best served by dealing with you and your company by drawing attention to testimonials that prove, via unbiased, satisfied clients, that you will make them look good. After all, the emotions that drive their purchasing decisions are at least as closely tied to their own personal interests as to those of their company.

Ratify and lock in the sale, by calling on the technique of verbal endorsement. As you restate clear-cut buyer benefits, using the Concern–Feature–Benefit progression, tie each one to their direct self-interest with:

- "This means that you will then be able to . . ."
- "As a result, your productivity and bottom line will improve dramatically . . ."
- "This can't help but make you look good, as the person who made the right decision . . ."
- "The obvious benefits to you are [list benefits].

Each of these "endorsements" helps you to "jump the desk" and to stimulate prospects to visualize for themselves the definite advantages of buying from you.

Sales Credit References

Bear in mind that none of your potential buyers would ship anything to a new customer without a credit check, and when they buy from an unknown vendor, they're looking for a supplier quality, reliability, and competitiveness check.

Shock-Value Verifying

If Verifying seems to be not much more than a rather boring extension of the Demonstration, consider the experience of an industrial salesman, who stumbled onto what he calls "Shock-Value Verifying" just prior to triumphantly Closing a very difficult sale.

He was selling a new line of polyvinyl chloride (PVC) industrial hoses when he made his first call on a distributor in Texas. As he gave his name to a counterman and asked for the sales manager, he imagined that the man gave him rather an odd look, and when he saw the expression on the sales manager's face as the latter introduced him to the firm's owner, he was sure that something was wrong.

After a few minutes of conversation about local business conditions and prospects for increasing his own firm's sales of PVC hose, the owner suddenly seemed to come to a decision as he slapped both palms on his desk, rose to his feet, and said, "Why don't you come with me?" Without another word, he led the way up three flights of stairs, with each floor being noticeably warmer than the one below, until, by the time they reached a big trap door blocking access to the fourth floor, it was stiflingly hot. The sales rep realized that, with outside temperatures in the nineties, heat was gathering at the top of the building. But this still didn't prepare him for the scene that met his eyes as the trap door swung open onto a huge, unventilated attic storage area, where the temperature must have been thirty degrees higher than outside. In the foreground, framed by neat tiers of shelving and barrels of nails, lay a dozen coils—or, more accurately, puddles—of melted plastic hose, with their pale, skeletal ribs of unmelted helix giving them the appearance of brightly-colored, but very dead, snakes.

Appalled as he was at this waste of good product, the rep firmly resisted the owner's attempts to "stick" him with thousands of dollars in "returns," and insisted that future hose shipments be stored under conditions that did not far exceed published heat tolerances for the product. That problem out of the way, he then put into effect his normal distributor-support program of paying visits to users along with distributor sales people, and enjoyed two days of writing big orders—until he was brought in to "convince" a big user, who had always bought rubber hose and wouldn't consider changing to the new, lighter, low-cost, plastic.

With this tough customer, the rep Linked carefully, established a solid Rapport, carefully Appraised the customer's needs, Demonstrated with a realistic hose-pressure test, and Verified with case histories that attested to successful use of PVC hose for water, sewage, fish, wine, milk, and wood-chip pumping in southern states. But still the user refused to be persuaded that the product would withstand Texas summer temperatures.

He was so adamant that plastic just couldn't do the job that the rep was about to admit defeat, when a sudden thought prompted him to ask the user to visit the nearby distributor with him, where he promised to settle the heat-tolerance question once and for all.

Two blocks, three flights of stairs, and one trap door later, they were so deep in conversation that the user was genuinely shocked when he was suddenly confronted with the multicolored puddles of melted hose, and it was a moment before he found his voice to ask how this disaster was supposed to prove that PVC was good for hot weather.

Cheerfully the rep pointed out that the mess they were looking at showed the user was right in his concern about potential heat problems, and then immediately went on to stress once more that, provided the hose was used with reasonable care in hot weather, this product was still hard-wearing, easy to handle, and definitely priced to save him money.

The user was still shaking his head in disbelief at this way of selling as he signed a big order for several styles of PVC hose. He became a firm convert to the product, *but* he always stored it in a cool area during the summer months.

Winning Actions and Attitudes

- **Make full and thoughtful use of the Fifth Pillar Affirmations for a week. Use them in conjunction with preceding ones.**
- **Address the serious problem of prospects who mistrust sales people.**
- **Obtain testimonials from every satisfied customer, and assemble case history material for future use.**
- **Be on the lookout for other forms of Verification that will strengthen your presentation.**
- **Reinforce, Reassure, Ratify.**
- **Verification and buyer-trust go hand-in-hand.**
- **Link requests for testimonials to requests for referrals.**
- **Your reputation is a vital element of Verification, so always remember that a bad reputation is gained in a moment and takes a lifetime to lose, while a good reputation takes a lifetime to build and is lost in a moment.**

THE SIXTH PILLAR/ THE SIXTH STEP AGREEMENT

Definition: Harmonize, Unite, Come to Terms, Fit, Match, Join Interests, Cooperate, Be of One Mind.
Key Affirmation: "I am able to establish strong bonds of empathy, warmth, and understanding—true *rapport* —with even the most difficult customer!"
Approximate Length of Step: 5 to 20 minutes.
Key Actions: Discuss 60 percent/Listen 40 percent.
Key Attitudes: The best agreement brings equal benefits to both parties.

Superprospect and the Unanswerable Objection

That's right, folks! To reach Agreement on the terms of the sale, Ordinary Sales Person will wrestle Superprospect, the intellectual giant armed with devastating new objections and expected to crush O.S.P. on the very brink of the sale!

Sounds ridiculous, doesn't it? And yet, this myth of the intimidating prospect armed with unanswerable objections is so ingrained in the U.S. sales psyche that a visit to the dentist compares favorably with trying to reach a sales Agreement.

Well, don't blink or the dreaded Superprospect may

turn back into an average buyer doing the best job she can for her company, and those fearsome 'new' objections, into the same old ones, dusted-off and framed in fresh phrases.

But why, after you have successfully countered a variety of objections in the course of the meeting, should any remaining ones suddenly assume such frightening proportions as the sale nears its climax? Consider that perhaps they are not genuine objections at all, but rather excuses masquerading as objections, and reflect the pressures felt by prospects as they approach a point of no return.

In selling, we first meet the early, often silent, approvals or objections by which prospects gauge our punctuality, appearance, handshake, attitude, phone call, or letter. Such critiques have unique importance, as it is the net sums of these incremental positive and negative estimates that divide average from outstanding sellers.

Then there are the objections that prospects use during the sale to assert control, and to fortify their understanding of what they are hearing. Finally, we encounter pseudo-objections, stalls, and excuses, which delay the Close, and which, by their nature, tend to be repetitious and hard to refute.

Scripted Replies to Tired Excuses

The reason we can sell for months without facing a single novel objection is that many prospects just keep on repeating the same old excuses to extract the lowest price, or to get rid of the sales person. The common basis of their rigidity is that they almost all:

- Fear making a mistake.
- Hesitate to disturb an existing cozy relationship with another supplier.
- Need more reassurance.
- Suffer from corporate "herd" indecision, which makes them avoid being the first to decide on a new vendor.
- Want you to visualize for them the success and approval from their decision to buy from you.

Worn out excuses are best handled with scripted responses. So note each objection as it arises, and commit your answer to memory. Try to respond to all comments or questions with your own open-ended queries. For example:

Prospect: "You won't be able to meet our delivery schedule!"

Sales: "What sort of deliveries are you looking for?"

Prospect: "Our present supplier gives us very good payment terms!"

Sales: "We can certainly discuss terms, if you don't mind explaining what you have in mind?"

Prospect: "The last time we changed suppliers, it was a disaster!"

Sales: "I think I know what you mean, but can you describe the problems you encountered? In this way, I'll make sure our people know what to look out for."

Each of these replies forces prospects to expand on, justify, and explain an objection. This method gets at the truth, and because of its directness, quickly puts an end to pseudo-objections and excuses.

Give Them Speaking Room

People may have difficulty expressing their true thoughts, but they still demand the chance to speak without interruption. No matter how outrageous their remarks or erroneous their positions, listen to them tactically and strategically, from a vantage point of warm, relaxed understanding and interest. Be objective and personally uninvolved, to keep discussions from turning into disputes. You certainly don't want the satisfaction of winning a battle, only to lose the war. There is no reason to fear objections, as they are milestones of your progress and the interest you have aroused. When they stop objecting, you have either lost them or they are getting ready to buy.

You Make the Buying Decision

When prospects are so obviously mired in indecision that they can't bring themselves to place the order, it sometimes becomes necessary to make the buying decision for them, as is illustrated by extracts from an article entitled "The Customer Wins When *You* Make the Buying Decision."

> "For many sales people, the most frustrating part of selling is the occasion when the customer agrees with everything you say, admits that your product is exactly what is needed, promises to buy, even outlines the size of a proposed purchase—and the order still fails to materialize.

"When this happens, and it seems that nothing more can be done, try looking beneath the surface, in order to understand what is preventing the customer from acting in his own, and your, best interest.

"Someone who simply cannot seem to implement a decision is often at the pull of opposing forces within his company—forces that conspire to gradually restrict his freedom of movement, until the ability to act is effectively neutralized.

"As a professional sales person, you may sympathize with, but you can never accept, the inaction of someone suffering from this problem. Instead, by taking the initiative in making the decision for a customer, you can often produce rewarding results for both parties.

"My company had been only semi-active in Western Canada for several years when I was given responsibility for this huge marketing area, and sales there were either flat or falling. We tried all the basic methods for reactivating the territory—improved sales support and product training, efforts to work more closely with key existing distributors, and the opening of carefully selected new ones. But it soon became clear that, although we were selling more old products to a shrinking heavy-industrial market, our new, high-tech items were not moving as they should, and we were mortgaging future growth by failing to respond to a rapidly changing economy. If something didn't change soon, we were about to receive a sharp lesson in the law of diminishing returns.

"The problem was most acute at our largest established distributor, who insisted on buying only older products and on working the same old markets, while refusing to consider positive changes. Fortunately, a new industrial sales manager was appointed, who saw what needed doing and who had authority to buy for his sales group. He promised to sell across our whole line while penetrating the emerging service economy, and plans were laid for large semi-annual stocking orders, for sales meetings and fieldwork, and for the setting-up of subdistribution throughout British Columbia.

"The Western Canada rep and I, feeling that our problems were solved, flew back to our respective offices to await the promised order.

"Weeks and months went by, filled with enthusiastic promises from this sales manager, but still no order—as the whole project grew colder and colder and the conflicting pressures under which he worked became apparent. Finally, having grown tired of making excuses to our company, the rep and I arranged for our regular year-end meeting with the distributor and were in the sales manager's office early the next morning.

"By pre-arrangement with the rep, our conversation throughout the meeting was kept deliberately as light and upbeat and as far from serious topics as possible, with no scramble at all to write the 'big order.'

"Lunch was not at the sales manager's usual restaurant. We wanted him to eat well, but not to feel too much at home. Again, the conversation was carefully steered to hockey and skiing, with only glancing references to business, and it was not until he had eaten dessert and was murmuring vaguely about 'getting back to the office' that we saw that the time had come to ask for the order.

"To make sure I was going to get my full say, as designated "hammer," we had seated him at the window-end of a booth, with the rep next to him and me directly opposite. To leave before we were ready, he would literally have had to climb over the table.

"Having decided to use the same hard tone learned in overcoming objections in telephone boiler-room selling, I waited for a lull in the conversation and said, 'Jim, we've guaranteed you everything you've asked for to get this line going in B.C., and we're all agreed about what needs to be done. We've had endless meetings and phone calls as we dance all around that big order you promised months ago. So, why don't we just go and write the order right *now*?'

"The effect on him of these few words was astonishing! The hand holding his cup shook enough to spill liquid on the tablecloth, and he went quite pale and gulped air for several seconds.

"Just as suddenly, the look of acute distress faded from his face, as the color returned to it. He straightened in his seat, drank down the rest of the coffee, placed the cup firmly in its saucer, and replied forcefully, 'Yes, let's *do* it!'

"Walking back to the office, he looked like a different man. All the doubt and indecision dropped away as he visibly regained the positive bearing that had originally so impressed us.

"We will always encounter waverers. Only now, having once determined where our joint interests lie, we should have no hesitation about assisting them to make up their minds—and most definitely when we know that the right purchasing decision will not only help us, but will make them look good too."

Final Objections

The "final" objection can suddenly appear like an unclimbable Mount Everest rising from a broad plain of easily-solved problems, an impasse that should be the last serious roadblock on an otherwise clear path to the Close. When confronted with one of these "head-knocking" situations, try throwing yourself on the prospect's mercy. Admit, with a minor apology, that you just don't have the answer, and ask how she would solve this problem if she were you.

In doing this, prospects are being appealed to on two distinct levels: as authorities, and as reasonable human beings. As authorities, as they will apply all their expertise to solving the problem; as reasonable human beings, they will tend to moderate their positions in trying to help solve it. Either way, the solution is in their hands, and they will not want it to escape.

Another way to "step into the buyer's shoes" when handling tough objections is to make use of "impartial" responses that "side" with prospects. For instance, an objection about having to buy a larger-than-wanted minimum order might prompt you to say, "I understand your concern. An account that I opened last month complained about the size of our minimum order too. But they soon realized that by doing business with us, they not only bought at better unit prices, but actually saved 20 percent on freight."

Here, the sales person begins by agreeing with a complaining prospect, and then enlists first the doubts and then the satisfaction of an unnamed, impartial customer to dispose of the objection.

Ethics and Reading Upside-Down

Just when it looks like smooth sailing to the Close, customers will occasionally subject sales people to a final integrity test that has nothing to do with the actual sale but is supposed to test the character of the sales person with whom they are thinking of doing business.

Reading upside-down may be an essential sales skill, but not necessarily when the buyer drops a competitor's quote on the desk within reach, and promptly leaves the room. Sneaking a peak at an unguarded "out" tray with the thought that the buyer wants you to see other vendors' prices may be valid and stupid and unethical, all at the same time.

The KGB had nothing on a purchasing agent acquaintance of mine, who once demonstrated to me how he could see and audio-tape everything sellers did in his office in his absence. Of one particular occasion, he said that it was both funny and pathetic to watch the "high-calibre" senior representative of a fine company glancing shiftily around to make sure he wasn't observed, then to hear him breathing heavily onto tape as he shuffled hurriedly through every file within reach. When his horrified young companion protested to him, he came over loud and clear remarking that these few minutes alone had made the whole call worthwhile, because now he was sure they'd get the business.

Not only did he not get that order, but his company was relegated from prime source to vendor of last resort as a direct result of his inability to play the game straight.

Buyers and purchasing agents do sometimes play "Drive the Price Down" by placing competitive information where you can steal a glance at it, or leaving the room so that you can have a good read. But don't allow yourself to be caught like this. If it's information that you should have, let them give it to you above board; if not, you're better off without it.

Play No Favorites

My grandfather, when walking with grandmother during the hard years of the Depression through a Picadilly Circus that swarmed with brazen "ladies of the evening," infuriated her by raising his hat to each one who accosted him. "They're just trollops and cheap tarts," she would rage, "and you degrade me by acknowledging them!" His reply was always the same. "They're all women, and as such, I must treat them with the same courtesy I would the Queen of England—or my wife."

The moral is, don't be either a snob or a sycophant as you sell. Big customers and small, switchboard operators, receptionists and secretaries, all deserve the same mannerly approach. Not just because it is good business, but because it is right, it builds your sales stature, and it pays continuous dividends. Many a sales person has been saved by a charitable word from a secretary, and for this reason alone it is wise to cultivate them as your closest allies. And remember that secretaries and receptionists can be promoted, and senior executives demoted, and none are more sensitive to slights than ambitious people on the way up, or has-beens on the way down!

Logic Has Its Place

As the structure of the sale is established on firm foundations of common interests, expressed needs, true Service, and honesty, it is time to strengthen the reasons for buying. Emotion, rather than logic, may prompt most people to buy, but confronted by "buyer's remorse," the fragile confidence born of emotion can evaporate like mist in the morning sun. The logic that couldn't make the sale comes into its own once the sale is made, as we realize that buyers need more than a "warm feeling" to support their commitment to a large purchase. Reinforce their emotional reasons for buying, but fortify them also with solid, logical, bottom-line reasons for giving you the order—reasons that carry them over moments of doubt and lock in the sale.

Winning Actions and Attitudes

- **"Live" the Sixth Pillar Affirmations as you combine them with others from the Positive Action Acronym, and design your own.**
- **Analyze, uncover, and annihilate objections.**
- **Script open-ended responses to pseudo-objections.**

- Give them warmth, compassion, understanding, and speaking room.
- You make the buying decision.
- Integrity and your reputation go hand-in-hand.
- Emotion plus logic is needed to lock in the sale.

THE SEVENTH PILLAR /THE SEVENTH STEP CLOSE

Definition: Bring to an end, Conclude, Unite, Finish, Terminate, Agree.

Key Affirmation: *"Service* is not just a seven-letter word, it is a central concept of my sales success and of the success of my customers!"

Approximate Length of Step: 5 to 10 minutes.

Key Actions: Question 50 percent/Listen 50 percent.

Key Attitudes: I close as I sell—ethically and honestly, with mutual profit in mind.

A Close to Remember

When I was seventeen, and waiting to go into the British Army, England being a very stuffy country, no one would give me a job for such a short time. So I travelled to the great South Coast resort town of Brighton, and got work as a beach photographer—what is known in the trade as a "smudger"—which gives some idea of the quality of the work.

My pitch, where I operated, was the best in town. It was on the Palace Pier, a magnificent, 100-year-old, cast-iron structure, reaching out a quarter of a mile into the English Channel towards France. I worked one side, and Charlie Pickrell the other. Charlie had been a beach photographer for more than thirty years,

and was one of the great gurus of "smudging." An acer-
bic, profane, chain-smoker, who was also a brilliant
salesman, he watched me for two days with growing
disgust, until he could stand it no longer. Then, without
warning, there he was, nudging me sharply with the
metal base-plate of the big "South Coast Reflex" camera we all used, and barking, " 'Ere"—he was far too
rude to use my name—" 'Ere, what's the biggest order
you've ever 'ad then?" Having forced from me the re-
luctant admission that my biggest order and my average order were both the same size as the smallest
order we were allowed to take—two black-and-white
postcards—Charlie made what were, for him, major
concessions. "You stop the people well," he said, "you
pose them nicely, and you don't take bad pictures, but
you have to be the very worst salesman I have ever laid
eyes on!" My defensive "I'm doing alright" produced a
triumphant, "Doing alright! You're *starving*!" This really
got my back up, so I shot back, "Okay, if you're so
flaming good, you show me how to do it!" Charlie considered for a moment, nodded, and ordered, "Right!
Stop this bunch behind you!"

I swung round to see a large, holiday group of ani-
mated Cockneys from the East End of London bearing
down on us. They all wore comic hats with "Kiss Me
Tony!" on the front and had their arms linked as they
did a sort of progressive cancan to a bellowed rendition
of, "Knees up Mother Brown! Knees up Mother Brown!
Knees up, Knees up, Don't get a Freeze Up! Knees up
Mother Brown!"

I knew from experience that these Cockneys, flush
with cash from hop-picking in Kent, were terrible prospects for photographs, due to their age-old mistrust of
outsiders. But with Charlie's stern gaze on me, there
was no escape, so I zeroed in on an imposing woman
who was obviously the herd leader.

"That's it, Madam," I yelled above the din. "Stop right

there! Don't let your holiday end without having a picture of you and the whole family! This'll be the photo of your life! That's it, stop just where you are!"

They finally stopped and allowed themselves to be posed on our life-sized stuffed donkey and our big stuffed lion, and held onto a six-foot papier-maché Guinness bottle. They really liked the bottle and got deeply involved with it. Then I made them all shout "cheese" together, took their picture, and immediately handed them over to Charlie Pickrell.

As a Londoner himself, Charlie had no trouble Linking with the group, or in overcoming their fears of being caught in yet another tourist-trap rip-off. Then he established a firm Rapport with individual group members, so that everyone was "sold," and found out that the "herd leader" liked sending postcards to her numerous grandchildren.

He involved her closely as he was getting her name and address down correctly on his pad, carefully checking spelling and pronunciation, and had begun to write the order, when his air of jolly friendliness was replaced by a decidedly forceful tone of voice. "Right, Madam! So we'll put you down for the FORTY-EIGHT postcards, or just the thirty-six!"

As his words sank in, she gasped and clutched at the nearest relative for support. "Oh, mate!," she cried desperately, "What am I goin' ter do wiv forty-eight postcards? I ain't got that many grandkids, an' I don't write that well!"

Instantly Charlie was at her side, a comforting arm around her shoulders. "Madam," he said, resuming his gentle tone, "don't you worry. Just for you, and because it's Saturday, we'll let you have the thirty-six."

And you know, she was so deeply relieved not to have to write forty-eight laborious postcards that she went on her way as happy as a sandboy.

From that day on, my average sale went up by a

factor of at least twelve. I commonly sold 24 postcards, lived very well, drove a second-hand "Jag," and started going out with older women. It was really the start of my sales training, and it is also a memorable example of an "Options" Close.

Ready, Set, Close

Afterwards, Charlie took care to explain that a key to his success in nearly always getting the order lay in his practice of never asking for it until he was sure that customers were ready to buy. When he said, "You've got to keep probing until they tell you they're ready," he really meant that persistence and the right open-ended questions will yield affirmative answers that show a clear readiness to buy. The news that several "grand-kids" would soon have birthdays told him that the grandmother was ripe to buy, and that he should now ask for the order.

Readiness-to-Buy Questions

- *"I'd like to get your comments on our discussion so far . . . ?"*
- *"Do you think option 'A' or option 'B' will work better for you . . . ?"*
- *"Who else do we need to talk to to get this project underway . . . ?"*
- *"How do you think my suggestions will help with your problems . . . ?"*
- *"What else do we need to talk about to complete this purchase . . . ?"*

- *"What else do we need to discuss that may be discouraging you from buying . . . ?"*
- *"When will you be making the final decision to buy . . . ?"*

Because these "readiness" questions confine themselves to the area of personal estimation and personal judgement, while carefully avoiding requests for hard purchasing decisions, affirmative replies to them indicate that it is time to ask for the order. Negative responses, on the other hand, are evidence of still-unresolved objections, which must be faced and dealt with before the sale can go through.

Confusion in the Close

As the only sales step universally recognized by buyers, as well as sellers, the Close has a special mystique, which can be confusing to customers and sales people alike. Much of the blame for this confusion must be shared by car dealers and high-pressure real estate operators for insinuating a special breed of persons, called "Closers," between sellers and prospects, to "get the order." This unnatural amputation of the final stage of the sale has had the effect of associating "Closing," in the public mind, with all known forms of duplicity and manipulation.

Sales people who understand how to sell can be trusted to complete the sale themselves, and don't need spurious proxies to do it for them. In fact, the pressures on these "Closers" to justify their existence have resulted in a proliferation of so-called "Closes," until they number in the hundreds. But of what real use are they, when a seller can only remember one or two at a time, or will have nothing to do with the threats, intimidation, greed, enticement, switch-and-bait, hypnotism, and outright lies implicit in many of them? The old saying "Liars need long memories" certainly applies to selling, and clearly shows that simple, honest Closes work best.

Simply Close

Good Closing isn't difficult or frightening when properly-trained sales people learn to Close throughout the sale. By closing stage by stage, closing one before moving to the next, as though each were one of a series of doors in a corridor called the sale, the whole process becomes a succession of logical minor Closes in preparation for the "big one" that results in an order.

Any experienced sales manager has horror stories of sitting in agony while an overzealous trainee rep talks his way into, through, and out the other side of a sale. And this is another objection to long, over-calculated Closes: Prospects who have been thoroughly prepared, during several previous stages, to decide in your favor, don't want to go through it all again. Once they've been brought to the point of buying, your only remaining responsibility is to help them express positive opinions and make a simple decision.

Paper-Trail Close

Let's suppose that the "paper trail" for your type of business starts with a standard written proposal, or with a purchase order, letter of intent, or contract. All of the key points in the appropriate document will have been agreed to by both parties to the sale, and now need only the validation of the buyer's signature. In this case, your easiest Close is probably just to ask prospects to sign the specific form that Closes the sale.

- *"As long as we've covered everything, I'll be happy to take a purchase order with me?"*
- *"If you approve of our proposal, perhaps you'd just initial it, so we can get the project under way?"*
- *"Would you like to look over the contract again before signing it?"*

Presuming the Close

Another popular way of Closing is to presume by your words that the sale is already made.

- *"So we'll have our people here early on Wednesday morning, to meet your Chief Engineer and get the project underway, unless Thursday would suit you better?"*
- *"Before we have lunch to celebrate this new contract, all we have to do is initial it!" (Sales person initials document and passes it to prospect for similar action.)*

More on the "Options" Close

We've already covered the tried and true Options Close, but here are one or two further illustrations.

- *"Will you have your car fully detailed inside and out, or would you prefer just an exterior wash and polish?"*
- *"I can offer you our fifteen-year fixed-rate mortgage, or the thirty-year variable with a slightly lower APR?"*

Golden Silence

When the time comes for you to Close, wait until there are no unnecessary distractions (don't try to compete with third-party interruptions or the telephone), look straight at the prospect, ask for the order, and then just SHUT UP!

Winning Actions and Attitudes

- **Make the Seventh Pillar Affirmations work for you as you review Affirmations for all the Pillars.**
- **Be sure they're ready to buy before asking for the order.**
- **There is nothing for you to fear in asking customers to decide in your favor.**
- **After you ask, silence is golden!**
- **You're the only "Closer" you'll ever need!**

PROFESSIONAL TELEPROSPECTING

All across America, telemarketers are on a roll, predicting nearly eight million new jobs in their industry by the end of the century—more than will be generated by any other in the same period of time. And with equal confidence, these same phone-sales prophets tell us that by the year 2000, we'll sell by telephone or we won't sell at all. But their arguments tend to downplay recent advances in the deregulated national communications network, which has only just begun to assemble the next generation of electronic communications marvels. They also fail to acknowledge that, as long as telephone calls engage only one of five human senses, this limitation alone is enough to spur radical changes in the medium.

In fact, available technology and the growth of video-conferencing allow us to predict that telemarketing, as we know it, will be fairly short-lived, and that within a few years it may be little more than a memory.

Video-Link Selling

It did not require genius to foresee the 1929 entertainment upheaval heralded by Al Jolson's "talkie" *The Jazz Singer*, which, with a few spoken words, destroyed the careers of a generation of silent-screen stars. Improvements in today's limited phone technology will inevitably produce a reverse communications revolution, to change or terminate the careers of thousands of telemarketers. Jeans-and-sneakers garbed telephone sales people will be just as shocked to find themselves suddenly "facing" their customers, as were John Gilbert's adoring fans at first sound of their idol's squeaky voice. And so, here we go again, right back to where we started, practicing the age-old skills of "face-to-face" selling—only this time via a video screen!

The largely artificial divisions between in-person sales and telemarketing, which seem to have been created so that the latter could be promoted as an activity having no connection to traditional selling, will disappear with a general return to "basics." But because telemarketing is now taught separately, we'll concentrate here on the telephone selling that is common to millions of in-person sellers—prospecting by phone for appointments.

Anatomy of the Call

The sale that opens with a telephone call and progresses through a personal meeting to an order is divided into two distinct parts.

Prospecting phone calls concern themselves with Linking, Rapport, and Appraisal, while later face-to-face meetings propel the sale through Demonstration, Verification, and Agreement to a Close. But the unavoidable delay between telephoning and meeting face-to-face makes it essential for the seller to run through an abbreviated version of the three "social" steps (Link, Rapport, Appraise) again at the beginning of every in person interview.

If this seems a little over-careful, try relaying some fairly detailed information by phone to the secretary

Telephone Prospecting

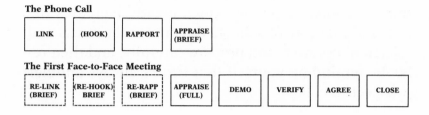

The Phone Call

LINK	(HOOK)	RAPPORT	APPRAISE (BRIEF)

The First Face-to-Face Meeting

RE-LINK (BRIEF)	(RE-HOOK) BRIEF	RE-RAPP (BRIEF)	APPRAISE (FULL)	DEMO	VERIFY	AGREE	CLOSE

for his or her boss, or transmit the same facts to the boss directly. Then, at the subsequent meeting, having first re-Linked and re-established Rapport, ask the first Appraisal question, "What do you know about my company and services?" The odds are that the buyer will reply either, "Nothing!", or come back with a misquoted version of what he thought he heard earlier. Trying to build on this sort of weak listening and uncertain comprehension can very easily lose you the sale.

Now is the time to confront the fact that most prospects just don't care whether or not you sell anything. Preoccupation with their own problems leaves them indifferent to your success, and adversely affects the way they hear, comprehend, and transmit what you tell them. This is especially true of telephone communications, when salient points are not imprinted with eye contact and body-language.

Telephone "Speed-Up"

Telephone-neutralizing of four out of five senses results in rapid, but often inaccurate, processing of information. In addition, telephone selling compresses sales time. Ten minutes face-to-face may equal only thirty seconds by phone, which greatly increases the strain of this way of selling. To counter the stress and rejection, research and prepare carefully, and then relax by reminding yourself that there's always another prospect to call.

Space, Equipment, and Planning

Take a leaf from the telemarketer's book by equipping yourself properly. Then plan your calls, prioritize your sales objectives, and discipline yourself to prospect by phone at the same time each day.

Telephone prospecting goes better when a special desk is reserved for it, and removing it from the general office clutter definitely makes it easier for you to do a professional job when you lift the receiver and start calling. Fit the phone with a twenty-foot spiral cord, to let you move around as you work—scooting smoothly from filing cabinet to PC to sample shelves. Physical movement helps to relieve tension, notably in the shoulders and neck, and standing up to deal with tough prospects can give the sales person a useful psychological advantage.

At the end of your telephone "shift," prepare a list of "A," "B," and "C" prioritized leads for the next day's calls, and, using a Daily Activity Sheet (see Appendix), list each prospective account, so that there is no excuse for breaking tomorrow's phone-prospecting schedule.

Telephone Selling Compresses Sales Line

Face-to-Face Meeting		Three- Dimensional		Extended "Processing" Time
SEE	HEAR	SMELL	TOUCH	INTUITION

Telephone Call	Two- Dimensional	Very Brief "Processing" Time
HEAR	INTUITION	

Establish Call Objectives

Before making that first call, again ask yourself that all-important question, "What am I selling?", including the reminder that it isn't just basic products and services. In phone prospecting, the Primary Objective is to sell an appointment to demonstrate goods or services. If you can't Close on an appointment, or are unable to reach the decision-maker, your Secondary Objective is to agree on a date and time to call again. Can't achieve that either? Then question in order to find the true degree of interest in what you sell, and set an approximate date—weeks or months away—to re-contact. Failing these three objectives, a fallback goal might be to determine if the prospect should go onto a new-products mailing list.

Call Progression

Most calls begin with the switchboard operator and then go through a secretary or assistant to the decision-maker, which means selling yourself, in slightly different ways, three times in succession. Sell yourself to the operator as part of a quest for information; to the secretary in order to dissolve her telephone "screen"; to the decision-maker before you can sell an appointment.

Of the three, the operator is your "window" onto prospective accounts. He or she is arguably the only person in the firm's "administrative chain" who is completely impartial about your success in penetrating the account. Many operators work alone as virtual switching devices, forwarding 300 or more calls a day. On a typical shift, they make many fleeting human contacts, but seldom enjoy a proper conversation with anyone. Theirs can be tough, unrewarding work, made much tougher by unhappy customers and pushy, insensitive sales people.

Make Friends with the Operator

Begin by making a friend of the operator. Don't just demand to know who buys office supplies, but treat her as the important human being she is. Say, "Good Morning! My name is ___ ___, with the ___ Company. Could you help me with some information, please?" (Speak deliberately, and don't worry about interruptions.) Follow this with, "I know you're very busy, so if you have to take another call, I'll just hang on until you can get back to me."

And because operators are so busy, be ready with specific questions that make good use of any time they can spare you.

- *"Can you tell me the name and title of the person who buys office supplies?"*
- *"How do you spell that name, please?"*
- *"Do I have to go through his secretary, or does he have a direct Centrex number?"*
- *"What's the earliest time I can catch him in the morning?"*
- *"Presumably he's out for lunch between noon and about one P.M., and isn't available much after five?"*
- *"In case I don't get through direct, what's his secretary's or assistant's name, and what time does she come in?"*
- *"I expect they stagger their lunch hours to keep the phones covered?"*

Between questions, and sometimes halfway through her response, the operator "disappears" to help other callers, comes back, and disappears again. And each time she does so, you get to know her a little better. Ask her name and how long she's worked there. Sympathize with her on the difficulties of her job, and be sure that at the end of the conversation your new friend will comment favorably about you to secretaries and decision-makers.

Use her name in thanking her for her help, and emphasize that you look forward to talking to her again soon. A note or phone call to her supervisor will lock her in as an active ally and future source of valuable information whenever you need it.

Call Strategy

As a result of your questions, you now know:

- The first and last names of the decision-maker and of his assistant or secretary, with proper spelling and pronunciation and their individual Centrex numbers.
- That he comes in at eight, eats lunch at his desk, answers the phone in his secretary's absence, and goes home at six.
- That she arrives at nine o'clock, lunches out from noon to one, and leaves at five-thirty.

If the secretary/assistant is the trained call "screen" you suspect, careful reconnaissance has revealed that you have a full two-and-a-half hours (8 to 9, 12 to 1, and 5:30 to 6) to bypass her and contact the decision-maker directly.

Dissolving the "Screen"

In selling "screens," the steps are Link, compressed-Rapport, and then "hook." Use a name Link before introducing yourself and your company, and after a quick Rapport-building follow-up, ask to speak to the decision-maker.

Some sales people skip the preamble and ask forcefully to speak to "Jack," or ask if "Jack is in," in the hope that the screen will be bluffed into putting a "friend" through without any questions. Okay if it works. But if it doesn't, you look shifty, and throw away the opportunity to build a relationship based on straightforwardness and trust.

When asked, "What is it about?", or "Can I say what this is in reference to?", relax (put a smile in your voice), and reply with a disarming, "Yes, of course!", or "I'm glad you asked that!" (and be *genuinely* glad), and then move into your concise, tightly-worded "hook."

Psychology of the "Hook"

The "hook" resembles a shortened version of the "statement of benefits" used by some in-person "scatter-gun" sellers when they should be listening or asking questions. Its effectiveness in telephone prospecting for appointments is ingrained in the screen's career-identification with the decision-maker. Her promotions, pay raises, and job prospects at this company are all closely-linked to his success, and the job of the hook is to push her into deciding that it is in both their interests to put you through.

When I am prospecting by phone, I never mention sales training because its association in their minds with some low-grade, in-house programs debases the value of my offering and is more likely to make secretaries hang up than forward my call.

Instead of fighting the screen, I'll relax, smile broadly into the little mirror on my desk, and reply, "I'm glad you mentioned that! Actually, my firm has identified four ways to dramatically improve sales performance and profitability for companies such as yours!"

There is hardly a company anywhere whose main concerns aren't summed up in what I have just said, and the screen knows this, because she takes the minutes at frequent top-level executive meetings, where these two topics are discussed in detail. My own 19-word hook relates directly to her interests, via the company and her boss, and prompts her to decide in my favor.

She'll tell me when to call again if the decision-maker is busy, and provided there's enough time between contacts, I'll send a postcard of thanks, which also serves as a reminder that I'll be calling.

> Dear Joan, Thank you so much for your help today! As arranged, I'll call Mr. Brown at exactly 3:30 P.M. on Friday. Perhaps you'd be kind enough to put this card in his desk diary as a reminder to expect my call? Again, Many Thanks. (signed) _____

A small added touch, but it really ups the contact rate!

Selling the Decision-Maker

When you finally get through to key players, confirm their identities as a way of leading into a name or other Link, give your name and company name, and pause to encourage them to respond. To the extent that they do, their fear and suspicion of you tend to be dissolved. Be alert for Negative Shared Experiences or other Linking opportunities to stimulate further comments, and in response to their questioning repeat the hook in the same relaxed way that worked so well with the screen.

To decision-makers, your hook says in a few words that you can help to solve their pressing problems, and it prepares them for the Appraisal.

Appraise

Phone Appraisals differ from face-to-face ones in that they cut out the "fluff" and concentrate on those Super Specific Needs Appraisal Questions that extract only the information you must have to sell an appointment. As prospects can't see how their answers are received, reinforce them with "Yes" and "Uh Huh," and ask them to speak a little more slowly so that you can get this important information down correctly. This bolsters their egos, and your professionalism in their eyes, and provides sellers with early opportunities to take unobtrusive command of the telephone call.

As soon as prospects have bought the hook and responded to open-ended needs questions, Closing on an appointment is not difficult. A presumed Close works well in this context as you ask, "Which day will be more convenient for us to meet, on Tuesday at 10:30, or would you prefer Thursday at 3:15?"

Accept the fact that you will not sell ten out of ten, and that it takes courage to control a developing situation and turn it to your advantage. Be prepared to stand your ground when screens or decision-makers ask for literature instead of forwarding your call or agreeing to a meeting. Tell them that you'll be happy to bring a brochure with you, but that you're the best advocate for these services, and that, in any case, they'll want to see you before doing business.

Don't be "conned" into long conversations with subordinates, particularly into giving too much information to screens. They can't buy, and the more information they have, the more likely that they'll lose you the appointment by transmitting it incorrectly. They often like to make decisions, and the more they know, the better qualified they think they are to give you the "thumbs down."

Winning Actions and Attitudes

- Prioritize leads A, B, or C the previous day.
- Careful preparation and understanding of what you're selling make the most of phone-selling opportunities.
- Establish and hold to call objectives.
- Sell yourself to operators, screens, and decision-makers, and then Close on the appointment.
- Link, Rapport, Appraise by phone. Demonstrate, Verify, Agree, Close in person.
- Work on that hook!
- Check your progress with the Daily Activity and Weekly Summary sheets.
- Working the numbers, there are always 10,000 new prospects who can say "Yes!" for every one who says "No!"

WINDOWS OF OPPORTUNITY I: SELLING THROUGH SPEAKING

In a highly competitive age, it is not enough just to go on making the same old sales calls. Instead, we have to find ways to rise above the competition and work smart, rather than hard, to sell more.

"Selling through Speaking" is one such promising "Window of Sales Opportunity" through which to promote yourself, your company, and your products.

Number One Fear

The *Book of Lists* shows public speaking to be number one on the chart of Americans' Top Ten Fears—ahead of death by drowning. But when you've managed to overcome this fear, and have assembled an interesting talk on something you've gained expertise in, you can find yourself addressing 50 or 100, or even 1,000 potential customers, and there is no sales efficiency quite like this!

Although anyone with sufficient courage can simply stand up and speak in public, for the sake of your reputation, it is usually better to "pay your dues" in mastering a demanding craft. Echoes of Chatauqua still linger to make America a speaker's paradise, but when its citizens are bombarded with two to five thousand print, radio, and television ads a day, we have to be good on the platform to be remembered.

Toastmasters Can Help

The would-be speakers' eternal riddle of how to find audiences when no one will listen to them until they are much better presenters than they are now, can be solved by joining a Toastmasters Club. This non-profit educational organization certainly qualifies as one of America's great, almost-free gifts to the world. For a few tax-deductible dollars a year, they will encourage you to talk your way through a ten-speech "basic manual," and several "advanced manuals," to become a Competent, Able, or Distinguished Toastmaster—all this while learning formal and impromptu speaking, as well as how to feel comfortable in front of an audience.

Toastmasters International, parent-body to over 6,200 clubs worldwide, is headquartered at P.O. Box 9052, Mission Viejo, CA 92690-7052, (714) 858-8255, and will send a free list of area clubs, if these are not advertised in local papers.

All clubs operate under the (non-discriminatory) Toastmasters International charter, and follow their very effective speaking program. Visit several as a guest before joining one. Select one that works hard to develop newer members.

Individual Toastmasters may spend two or three years learning the verbal skills so essential to success in this Communications Age, and then leave to practice them elsewhere, or they maintain active club memberships in order to sharpen those skills throughout their business lives.

Benefits of Selling through Speaking

Potential Client Contacts By Phone/ In Person

5 Contacts per Day × 250 Selling Days per Year	Contacts = 1,250

Public Speaking

1 Talk per Week (Audience 20 to 100 People) × 50 Weeks	Contacts 1,000 TO = 5,000

Sales people benefit greatly from a program that helps them to think and express themselves more clearly in speech and writing, while becoming more sensitive to the difficulties of others in voicing their thoughts. They practice management and leadership by taking part in the running of clubs and programs, and enjoy greater self-confidence and increased sales as forceful presenters and communicators.

Speaking to Service Clubs

If you already express yourself well and are a fairly confident speaker who just needs more practice or wants to try out new material without risking "bombing" in front of important prospects, contact the "service" clubs. Lions, Rotarians, Elks, and Kiwanians generally meet once a week to hear progress reports on their charitable projects, eat, present awards, and listen to a speaker.

These clubs "chew up" fifty speakers a year, and their members have heard so many good, bad, or indifferent talks that they make tough, hard-to-impress audiences. Because clubs want to feed their members and get them back to work in good time, they usually limit talks to about 25 minutes. They generally favor topics of business interest, and look for a speaker who presents him or herself well. Clubs rarely pay for talks, but are generous with meals, certificates of thanks, and testimonial letters.

Good speakers make useful contacts at these outings and find that they are passed from club to club as long as they keep to "time" and *never* try to sell in an obvious way from the platform.

Preparing a Speech

This is by far the hardest part of the whole project. Even highly paid professionals admit that on a speech's first airing it can easily take two or three *hours* of research and practice for every *minute* spent behind the microphone. For most newcomers, who have no idea where to begin, assembling an interesting talk can be a daunting prospect.

Given the right topic, just how does one stretch or squeeze a speech to fit all time-frames, from 5 minutes (Toastmasters), 45 to 60 minutes (after lunch), or 60 to 90 minutes (after dinner), without having to rewrite it every time?

Analysis of effective speeches reveals that the best

of them convey solid information wrapped in a series of stories or humorous anecdotes. And that's the secret. Construct the talk from one or more information-filled anecdotes, lasting an average of five minutes each, and containing a little humor whenever possible, often directed at yourself. Not Saturday Night Live belly laughs, but cameos from life's common joys and pains, which leave audiences chuckling, but not necessarily rolling in the aisles. Have a strong opening module, a "body" consisting of several more, and another powerful one for the close.

This modular construction is almost infinitely adaptable and takes more of the stress out of speaking. Seasoned pros or raw novices, it lets speakers remain poised and calm as they adjust easily to programs that run early or late, and to organizer's constantly changing demands.

A forty-five minute presentation contains 9 five-minute modules, an hour 12, and so on, so that you simply add or subtract units as the occasion requires. It's very important to have more modules available than are needed, and always to leave the opening and close modules intact.

When audience alertness and comprehension are compared to a horizontal sine wave pattern, the anecdotal presentation style enables speakers to "grab" participants' attention and raise it to a peak. Minutes later, as their alertness is nearing the bottom of a trough, another short story serves to lift it to new heights.

Providing valuable information through realistic short stories and humor works well with today's audiences, who have been visually conditioned by television. They will not sit through boring recitations of bare facts; they demand to be entertained with vivid verbal pictures that they can "process" and immediately convert to their own use.

As a sales speaker, you are "selling" listeners on buying your concepts, so encourage their natural desire to participate in presentations. Their enthusiastic involvement enlists them in your sales force to sell themselves on the ideas you're conveying.

Know That They'll Like Your Talk

Speakers, not knowing what an audience wants to hear, or how they'll be received, suffer needlessly from pre-event anxiety, for they have two simple ways to make sure that their talk will be well-focussed and well-received. Reading and researching all available facts on the listener group is one way. This helps the speaker to avoid unpleasant surprises. But it is no substitute for a Needs Appraisal meeting with the organizer, followed by phone calls to individual audience members.

Ask meeting planners for the names and telephone numbers of five to ten people representing all age and experience levels within the audience, and contact them by telephone about two weeks before you're booked to speak. My own interviews of audience members use scripted questions, so that nothing is missed: "What sales training have you had?" / "Have you attended a sales seminar recently?" / "What do you hope to get out of my talk?" The timing of these calls creates interest in the topic, and kills several other birds with one stone.

- Answers to my questions enable me to zero in on audience concerns, so that from the first words, they feel as comfortable with me as I do with them.

- These calls provide background material and humorous "color" for the talk, especially when I ask interviewees, "What's the strangest, or funniest, selling experience you've ever had?"
- Interviewees become my friends in the audience, who also help to "fill the room" by telling their peers about this speaker who cares enough to solicit their opinions.
- The presence of these individuals draws me closer to the audience when I cite their responses and refer to them by name during the talk.
- They provide a reliable pool of positive questions and comments.
- They are the first to approach me after the presentation, which fosters the aura of success, and breaks down the reserve of others who would like to ask questions and enroll for further training.

Evaluating a Speech or Seminar

Speakers should record every talk, and then use the resulting audio or video tapes to improve their presentation. It helps if they also obtain objective evaluations from their audiences.

Always include an evaluation sheet with other program handouts. The sample evaluation sheet here, the result of many revisions, can be quickly and easily completed, while still leaving plenty of room at the bottom for business-building referrals. After all, the least you can do when asking audiences for the favor of a written critique, is to reduce it to a simple, single-sided sheet.

Speech/Seminar Evaluation

	Excellent	Good	Fair	Poor
Purpose of presentation was clear:	—	—	—	—
Presentation helped me to understand topic:	—	—	—	—
Quality of information provided:	—	—	—	—
Speaker was effective in communicating the subject:	—	—	—	—

Comments: _____
_____
_____
_____
_____

I feel the following people would like to hear about your speeches/seminars. Please tell them _____ suggested you contact them. (your name)

Name: _____ Phone ( ) _____
Company: _____ Title: _____

Name: _____   Phone (   ) _____
Company: _____   Title: _____
Name: _____   Phone (   ) _____
Company: _____   Title: _____

Stressing the importance of participants' comments on various aspects of your presentation encourages them to view themselves as authorities (and to complete the evaluation).

Finally, to paraphrase Bill Gove, one of America's great speakers: "Remember that 25 percent of them will love you, and 25 percent will hate you, no matter what you do. Knowing this allows you to focus on converting the remaining 50 percent." It also makes the occasional really cruel comment easier to bear.

The Rewards of Speaking

Sales people who take every chance to handle sales and product training for their companies, and who sell by speaking to industry audiences, automatically set themselves above their peers in the minds of their superiors. They tend to receive better pay raises and promotions, and as they are seen by customers as having much greater knowledge and authority than their competitors, are likely to be rewarded with larger and more frequent orders.

So, if you've been wondering how to break out of a sales rut, and how to raise your visibility and prestige in the eyes of your company and customers, start thinking about how *you* can sell through speaking.

Winning Actions and Attitudes

- Break out of that selling rut!
- Join Toastmasters, choose your speaking topic, explore "service" clubs, and start speaking.
- Join and speak to organizations frequented by prospects.
- Use the easy, powerful modular speech construction.
- Write your own (*maximum 1 minute*) introduction, mentioning what it is that you sell. Enlarge it on a copy machine for easy reading in poor light.
- Arrive early to check house microphone, sound-balance, lectern, lighting—in time to make needed corrections.
- For fastest improvement, record *everything*. For saleable-quality tapes, use a Panasonic RQ 382 *Auto Reverse* Standard Cassette Recorder, coupled to a Radio Shack Tie Pin Mike (Catalogue #33-1063). Carry the recorder in pocket or purse, or wear it on a belt in a Coaststar accessory case (available from camera stores).
- Market yourself to other organizations with testimonial letters from earlier talks.
- Make selling through speaking an important part of your business plan.

WINDOWS OF OPPORTUNITY 2: SELLING THROUGH WRITING

"Windows of Sales Opportunity" are identified by their capacity to jolt sellers out of work ruts, boost efficiency, bring in fresh customers, expose new markets. Under any of these criteria, "Selling Through Writing" qualifies with flying colors!

Articles carrying your byline reach out into sales unknown to uncover exciting new markets, and touch hundreds or thousands of prime prospects who might otherwise never hear of you. Unfortunately, unpleasant associations with staying after school to make 500 copies of "I will not talk in class," and a lack of practice since then, conspire to keep all but a few of us from getting into print to increase sales.

But writing need not be alarming or difficult. Anyone who can write an acceptable business letter is capable of marshalling facts to form the basis of a short "filler," a quiz, or an article. And with new trade and professional publications coming out all the time, demand for all types of material is rising steadily.

Find the Right Vehicle

Ask customers which professional publications they subscribe to, and go through industry magazines to find interesting subjects about which you feel you could write. Next call their editors to "float" article ideas, and if they respond positively, ask for several sample magazine issues and a copy of their "Editorial Guidelines."

Now study the guidelines to familiarize yourself with:

- Publication dates
- Readership makeup, education levels, and average incomes
- Other publications to which the readers subscribe
- Readers' main interests
- The writing style, layout, and article length editors prefer

Then read and reread the sample issues, to immerse yourself in and get a real feel for the publication.

Finally, find the appropriate section in *Writer's Market* (F & W Books, 1507 Dana Ave, Cincinnati, OH 45207), and research this excellent source for other markets for your work.

Questionnaire, Filler, or Article?

With a topic decided on, and clear reader and publication profiles in mind, it's now time to pick a "format" to get you quickly into print. If writing a full-length article still boggles your mind, begin with a short questionnaire. Readers and editors love them, and because they're only a few sentences strung together, are very easy to write. They also offer double-mileage when written first from a buyer's and then from a seller's perspective.

Questionnaire for Buyers:	"Ten Key Things to Look For Before Buying a New _____!"
Questionnaire for Sellers:	"Sell more _____ When You Tell Prospects What They Want to Hear!"

From questionnaires, progress to a 50- or 100- word "filler" containing an information-nugget readers can clip out, store in a purse or wallet, and put to immediate use. With the growth of your self-confidence and writing ability, move up to 250-, 500-, or 1000-word articles.

Benefits of Selling through Writing

Potential Client Contacts By Phone/ In Person

5 Contacts per Day × 250 Selling Days per Year	Contacts = 1,250

Writing

1 Article per Week (1,000 to 20,000 Readers) × 50 Weeks	Contacts 50,000 TO = 1,000,000

Writing Style

Try a simple, anecdotal style of writing, similar to that which works so well for speakers; or you can elect to be a "problem-solver." Using the second technique, the writer describes a current, industry-wide problem, and the difficulties it has caused him or someone he knows. Then he shows how to solve it and draws helpful lessons for readers from the experiences he's described.

Either style lends itself to a natural, easy progression—from the "opening," through the "body" of the article, to the "close"—which has definite advantages for beginning writers.

Submitting Articles

Before clean-typing and sending in your contribution, consult *Writer's Market* again about manuscript layout, copyright protection, cover letters and fees.

If the magazine offers either a fee or a "bio-box" in lieu, take the second option for its promotional value. Write a 25- to 35-word "bio" (in the third person singular), giving your name, your company and its specialities, your address and phone number. Experience has shown that interested readers will write or call authors at once if they have an easily accessible address or telephone number. Lacking this information, they rarely take the trouble to contact them through the editor.

Always include a black-and-white glossy portrait photo with the "bio," and request its publication with the article. Seeing your picture gives readers a feeling that they know you and helps them to recognize you at meetings and conventions.

Contributing Editor

As you establish yourself as a regular contributor, and readers react favorably to your writing, ask the editor to list you in the publication's editorial information as a "Contributing Editor." If he says "Yes," request some business cards to go with this honorary, unpaid position.

As the world's greatest "door-opener," this new title will allow you to break through previously impregnable phone "screens," by announcing yourself as, "_____ _____, Contributing Editor for _____ Magazine!", who is calling the decision-maker to ask his opinion on a proposed article.

Soon, you'll be on first-name, soft-sell terms with CEO's of major corporations, who would never have taken your calls before.

Winning Actions and Attitudes

- **Read widely to broaden your information base.**
- **Create files for clippings that provide ideas for potential articles.**
- **Take 60 minutes today to write a first "quiz" that will get you into print!**
- **Interest prospects and customers with copies of your articles, enclosed with sales letters.**
- **Use copies of your articles as potent Verification material in face-to-face selling.**
- **Start writing today!!**

SALES
ENTERTAINING:
THE EATING
MEETING

Every year, American companies budget billions of dollars for entertaining customers—dollars that are largely tax-deductible and that support a large part of the U.S. hotel and restaurant industry.

But ask sales people how all these entertainment dollars are supposed to transform themselves into tangible purchase orders, and most will mumble vaguely about having to entertain customers because their competitors do, or because prospects and customers expect it. Very few know how to turn some half-formed theory of selling-through-entertaining into solid sales increases.

If selling is a science, then its entertainment aspects should be practiced scientifically too, and these aspects are only really justified when they serve clear-cut sales objectives with measurable results.

Whenever you entertain clients, you are really buying access to them and paying for their undivided attention. Expense-account sales people who ignore these facts in their pursuit of free meals soon find their cholesterol levels rising faster than their sales.

The Ultimate Soft Sell

Sales entertaining constitutes the ultimate soft sell; an occasion for carefully reviewing sales goals for an account (before issuing an invitation), and then putting all further thoughts of selling out of mind. By setting aside the burden of having to sell during the meal, theatre or sporting event, you are better able to break the security and routine of customers' working environments. Lifting work pressures and removing distractions allows them to relax, enjoy themselves, and reveal previously hidden personality facets that help you get to know the "real" person, and judge exactly how to sell them.

Some buyers eat at the same restaurant every day with one sales person or another—a classic example of the sales person surrendering control of the meeting to the buyer. You'll know you're in the wrong place when you find yourself trailing along behind your guest as she pauses to chat with colleagues and your fiercest competitors, and receives the homage waiters reserve for very special customers on the way to her "usual" table.

You are paying for her undivided attention, but far from opening up, she will watch every word for fear of being overheard, and later will use your presence to pressure those competitors into lowering their prices. In effect, you have paid heavily for the pleasure of being used to whipsaw their margins and yours.

Setting the Scene and Taking Control

Before issuing an invitation, find out where the buyer usually eats, and protect yourself by reserving a table at a good restaurant some distance away in the opposite direction. Anticipate objections with, "We'll go to a very nice place not far from here. The food is excellent, and the service is outstanding—I know you'll enjoy it!"

Call or visit the restaurant beforehand, to stress the importance of a good table, food, and service—if they want your business. Give the maitre d' your credit card number and the percentage you tip, so that a computed bill arrives unobtrusively at the table, needing only a signature, and causing no distraction for your guests.

Make it clear that the waiter is to take instructions only from you. This means that *you* ask your guests what they would like to eat and drink, and then convey their preferences to the waiter with your own order. This enables you to exert immediate control of the meeting in a way that is imperceptible, as well as socially correct, even if it does conflict with your previous, less-effective entertainment style. In an age of ill-trained and undisciplined waiters, you may have to ask for one who knows and will follow the proper etiquette.

Always arrange to meet contacts at their offices, and escort them to the eating place. Good manners and good strategy demand this courtesy, which also reduces the possibility of delays, cancellations, or mistaken addresses.

Moving to a "Social" Rapport

Chamelon-like, people change as they enter their daily business environment, to take on the "coloration" of their company. Ever failed to recognize at the supermarket someone who is a familiar figure in business? Then you'll know why it is so important to use the journey to the restaurant to "move" your guest from a working to a social rapport.

Buyers know that you are footing the bill in the hope of influencing a purchasing decision and are resigned to eating with someone who bends their ear throughout the meal. They brace themselves for the familiar onslaught and are all the more relieved and grateful when you not only avoid mentioning business, but actually redirect the conversation when they feel obliged to bring it up. Managing the meal in this way, as a practiced and solicitous host, creates strong positive impressions on customers that will have a favorable effect on this and future sales to their company.

Conversational Generalist

Entertaining can be very hard work if guests lack small talk, and leave you to carry the whole conversation as well as your other duties as host. Happily, all but the dullest will eventually respond as you probe gently for their interests and hobbies. This is where conversational "generalists" really come into their own, with their carefully cultivated ability to "prime the pump" with stimulating comments on wide-ranging subjects. A friend of mine, whose successful sales career depends largely on his sophisticated entertainment skills, remembers struggling desperately to find the right topic for a particularly bovine prospect, who greeted every remark with a stare and a grunt. Tired of chattering to himself, this salesman finally gave up and concentrated on his food. After a quiet half hour, disturbed only be the muted clink of cutlery, his guest took a final sip of coffee, pushed his chair away from the table, and without warning, began to speak. For the next hour, almost without drawing breath, he talked about politics, business, the environment, and space exploration. It quickly became clear that he was actually a brilliant conversationalist—just one who liked to anticipate and eat his meals in silence.

More on Control

The "eating meeting" is first and last a career-impacting business meeting, pleasant but not for pleasure, and a showcase for your social expertise, during which you need to listen, be alert, and keep your wits about you. Don't feel that you have to match guests drink for drink because guzzling alcohol rarely makes for profitable entertaining, and when people see that you aren't drinking, a surprisingly high percentage are relieved not to have to either. When dealing with a customer with a recognized alcohol problem, take control by quietly asking the waiter not to offer more than two drinks.

A few words of caution. Before his unfortunate end in one of New York City's great hospitals, Andy Warhol promised us each fifteen minutes of fame in our lifetimes. But to people who are routinely ignored by business associates, friends, and family, even this begins to seem exaggerated. Basking in the unaccustomed warmth of your attentive interest, customers may try to tell you more about their personal lives than you want to know—details that will embarrass them later and can make them hesitate to see you again. Deflect talk of illness, marital, career and financial difficulties with comforting, upbeat comments that steer the conversation over to positive, or at least neutral, areas. You certainly don't want them associating you with anything negative or depressing.

After the meal, escort them back to their buildings, but not to their individual offices. Buyers dread and deeply resent sales people who trade on their hospitality to force after-lunch selling sessions.

The "eating meeting" is the most frequent form of sales entertaining, but whether you buy lunch for prospects, or take big customers to sporting events, the theatre, or on hunting trips, the rules remain the same: Forget trying to sell, and concentrate on being an outstanding host.

How It Works

By accepting your choice of restaurant, prospects have broken the habit mold and are more likely to break it again to buy from you. They are profoundly impressed by your courtesy, your easy management of the meeting in all its details, and particularly with the warm personal interest taken in them. Such entertaining without obvious selling proves to prospects and customers that you are more concerned with forming a worthwhile long-term business relationship than getting an order, and helps them to think of you as a friend.

They will reward you by sending business and referrals your way, and by recommending your company. They'll also welcome your next contact, and guarantee you easy access when you invite them to lunch. Low-key, delayed-action selling it may be, but sales people who try it are often surprised at how this way of entertaining results in unexpected purchase orders in the next day's mail.

Winning Actions and Attitudes

- Check account-goals, and then forget about selling.
- Pick the restaurant, set the scene, move to "social" rapport.
- Concentrate on guests and use "generalist" conversational skills.
- It may take time for low-key selling to get results.

FIVE SPECIAL SALES TOPICS

Following are lists of "Power Points" to dramatically improve your PRODUCT/SALES TRAINING SESSIONS, STAND-UP PRESENTATIONS TO BUYING GROUPS, SALES LETTERS, DRESS, AND TRAVEL.

Product/Sales Training Sessions

No sales person qualifies as a fully-trained professional unless he or she can manage and conduct powerful product/sales training sessions. These meetings have much in common with public speaking, but make their own particular demands.

- Prepare presentation carefully, practice privately and then in front of people—especially if more than one person is presenting.
- Ship more materials than will be needed, in plenty of time for the meeting.
- One hour presentation *maximum*. Run longer, and you'll "lose" sales people who endure a sales meeting per week.
- Work point-by-point through a *brief* outline, copies of which have been given to the audience. There should be plenty of room for note-taking.

- Cover product training first, telling reps only what they need to know to sell the line.
- Use lightweight, easy-to-use "demos" that can be easily carried on sales calls.
- Coordinate the sales-training part of the program with the company's PR and advertising, and stress the support these give sellers.
- In highly-effective "team" presentations, one person introduces self, company, product or service, and team-mate. Second person then alternates with first to present successive parts of program. Changes of voice, approach, and alternating "sprint" segments hold energy, interest, and comprehension at high levels.
- DON'T patronize, talk down, talk too technically, compare their results with others', use "canned" films or slides, or demand too much.
- DO ask what they need to know, ask for their help, put yourself in their shoes. Involve them in role-playing, discussion, use of demos.
- Stress profits, ease of sales, benefits. Avoid product or service features unless they relate to selling, especially in new markets.
- Build to a climax, and finish *early*!

Stand-Up Presentations to Buying Groups

Toastmasters (and lots of practice) will help sellers to prepare for the modern phenomenon of selling to buying groups. There's nothing to fear as long as you:

- Prepare carefully, drawing on appropriate hints from PRODUCT/SALES TRAINING SESSIONS, with a view to controlling the presentation from its outset. Obviously this is harder to do with groups than individuals.

- Arrive early to position and test audiovisual equipment. Check that lighting is either overhead or behind you. Greet each group member as your company's guest.
- Greet all participants individually, and obtain their business cards as they enter. Arrange cards on table in front of you, to match seating arrangement, so you can address everyone by name.
- Link, Rapport, Appraise, and ask them questions, before starting the presentation.
- Present only with the primary decision-maker in the room.
- Identify subsidiary decision-makers, "white hats" and "black hats." Note the names of "pros" and "contras" on their business cards during the presentation.
- Arrange for a second person to share the presentation, help maintain control, and ensure that there are no neglected participants, or awkward silences. Decide beforehand which of the two of you will be in charge.
- Provide a short written summary for everyone, with space for notes.
- Present all information in terms of customer's interests and benefits.
- Keep presentation brief, ask for questions, answer briefly, and agree on the next action for both sides, to move the sale forward.
- Don't allow anyone but the primary decision-maker to monopolize the conversation. Include everyone in the discussion.

- Don't argue, but willingly deal with all objections.
- If you are to prepare a formal proposal, agree that you will meet with them again to go over it point-by-point, and serve as its advocate.
- Shake hands and engage eye-contact with each individual as you thank them for attending.

Sales Letters That Sell

Selling Through Writing is often a matter of stretching a limited idea to fit a 1,000-word article. By contrast, sales letters usually require the packing of a lot of information into one or two pages.

- Limit sales letters to one page where possible, as most people won't bother to read a second sheet.
- Keep them focussed, with active words and phrases, easily-understood terms—in short, attention-grabbing sentences and paragraphs.
- Use verbal "persuaders": Profit, Free, New, Guaranteed, Save Time, Save Money, Easy, Proven, Exciting, Yes, "You" and "We" rather than "I".
- Appeal to prospects' emotions by emphasizing the benefits they will receive as a result of using your services. Avoid the coldly logical approach of long lists of product features.
- Get in sync with customers by first acknowledging what they already know, and then addressing what they need you to tell them.
- Prove that you can meet their needs by referring to satisfied customers.

- Tell them what you'll be doing next (to move the sale towards the Close), and prompt them to action by announcing how and when you'll be following-up.

Proposal Format

A) A Proposal prepared for _____
   Title _____ Dept _____
   Company _____
   By _____
B) Refer to meeting/phone conversation. Thank person for seeing/talking to you.
C) Recap the needs/problems/wants points agreed on.
D) Mention features that match, and benefits that meet these expressed needs.
E) Summarize the positive results to be expected from the benefits you offer.
F) Outline actions to be taken by both parties.
G) Cost breakdown (on separate sheet).
H) Thanks, salutations, initials (box), date.

Dressed to Sell

Without getting into the details of *what* to wear when selling, here are a few guidelines to help ambitious sales people coordinate their clothes with their careers.

- Apply A, B, and C priorities to your clothes. Ignore the Bs and Cs and dress *slightly* above the sartorial levels of your most important A contact of the day.

- Never dress "down" to blue-collar prospects (small business owners, municipal employees), as they very often look up to the sales profession and expect sellers' appearances to match this image.
- Buying a few of the highest-quality classically styled clothes you can afford is preferable to owning a large wardrobe of quickly-dated, lower-quality clothing. Take it easy on the jewelry; too many rings and chains can offend more conservative customers.
- Keep in mind that promotions and pay increases are closely linked to the image you project. And people in their 40s, 50s, and 60s make the decisions at many companies.
- Pay special attention to hair, hands, briefcase, and shoes—all "eye-stoppers" to which your movements draw attention and on which customers' gaze rests.
- Natural fibres tend to wrinkle, and artificial ones to shine. Blends can offer the best of both worlds.
- Customers want to feel as comfortable with the appearances of sales people as they do with their products and services. To rise from selling low-level buyers in the basement, to CEO's in the corporate penthouse, clothing and accessories must keep pace with sales ability.

Travel to Sell

Sales people who travel a lot on business complain of gaining weight, losing physical condition, drinking too much, sleeping badly, and being exhausted by the time they get home. Regularly repeated, this cycle can seriously affect health and wreck family relationships. Sellers need to recognize that "long distance" selling *is* very tiring, and to take steps to maintain their health, while increasing their energy and sales, away from home.

- Leave home early on sales trips (perhaps on Sunday), and try to travel "off-peak" to arrive fresh and ready to sell.
- Join at least one airline "club," to avoid standing in so many airport lines, and to have somewhere reasonably quiet to work.
- Stay at the best hotel you can, and request in advance the room and floor you prefer. Hotels can perform miracles for regular guests who won't take "no" for an answer.
- Start and finish work earlier than usual, so that calls and reports are completed by mid-afternoon. Take a fifteen-minute nap lying flat on your back on the floor or on your bed, and breathe with your diaphragm. Do half an hour's calisthenics, followed by a thirty-minute walk or swim, and dine and go to bed fairly early.
- Avoid digestion-ruining fast food, and keep a special notebook for listing every exceptional coffee shop and restaurant in your territory, so that you're never at a loss for somewhere to eat well—and healthily!
- Handle travel "dislocation" (and avoid spending too much time in bars searching for company) by carrying with you a favorite book or small, relaxing project from home, to provide continuity and a sense of comfort.
- Call home before, rather than after, work, and ask family members to "hold" all but emer-

gency problems until you get back. You'll sleep better as a result.

- Let the family know that you may need an hour or two by yourself to unwind after your return from a difficult trip.
- Even if it isn't part of your contract, try to take half a day off for every week on the road.

Sales people following this trip formula will sell more, as they enjoy travelling, and will come back in better shape than when they left. They'll have better family lives, and will be able to maintain a tough travel schedule indefinitely without any ill effects.

DYNAMIC SALES SELF-MANAGEMENT

The 80–20 rule of selling, which applies to all products and industries, shows that, with the same levels of support and training, 20 percent of sales people will make 80 percent of sales—while a desperate 80 percent of sellers struggle endlessly to write the remaining 20 percent of the orders. In other words, a few sales people enjoy lives of outstanding prosperity and achievement, while many more with equal qualifications are condemned to lifelong low rewards.

There is no magic secret to consistent success in selling, but, just as "one sales pro always recognizes another," there *is* a special "attitude" to the business of sales that can virtually guarantee a "top twenty" selling career.

This special attitude can be detected at the job interview, in the successful sales person's relationships with management and other sales people, and in his planning and organization of sales in a territory.

Getting the Job

One of life's great mysteries is why accomplished sales people who could, as the saying goes, "sell a vacuum cleaner to a Bedouin," present their own qualifications so badly at job interviews. If they will just use the Seven Steps, with themselves as the product, they will not only get the position, they'll be able to hold their "price" in terms of salary, commission, and benefits.

On first contact with a prospective employer, ask for all available information on the company, so that you can be fully prepared for the interview. Annual reports, in-house newsletters, PR releases, newspaper articles, and business–library research will provide the background for a powerful, informed personal presentation.

The Interview

Dress carefully, arrive early, and be prepared to listen far more than you talk. Read trade magazines in the waiting area, to bring yourself up to speed on current industry concerns, and observe traffic around "reception," to see how the company handles customers and other sales people.

Open the interview with a name, traffic or weather Link, before moving into a Rapport built on your research and on industry information from the trade magazines.

When the interviewer is comfortably aware of your genuine interest in the company's concerns, rather than your own, progress to Super-Specific Needs Appraisal Questions that are also based on that earlier research. Write down all answers, to communicate that you recognize their importance, and to be sure that nothing is missed later in Agreeing on terms of employment. The higher the quality of the Appraisal, the fewer unpleasant surprises later on.

Demonstrate by reviewing sales accomplishments, and Verify with supporting testimonials, sales figures, and other hard evidence that what you've said is true. Encourage interviewers to sell themselves on employing you, by involving them in handling and commenting on each exhibit.

Get It in Writing

Sales is the engine driving the U.S. economy and every corporation within it, and as such touches every company employee, from product designer to shipping clerk, from CEO to custodial worker. And this complexity makes it essential for you to have a written Agreement with any new employer. Letter of intent, or formal contract—it must show salary, bonus, profit sharing, commission rates, and commission "splits" (when orders originating in one territory are shipped or billed to another). Agree that you will receive copies of all commissionable invoices for the territory as it is outlined geographically in the Agreement, and insist on a clear and fair definition of "house" accounts (accounts in your territory that are handled by the "house" or company, and do not pay you any commission).

The Equity Principle

The greater your success, the more likely you will be given the "opportunity" to open up new areas, while your developed and profitable territory is reassigned to an account-maintenance person who wouldn't know a sale if he fell over it. Talented account-openers are the most valuable of all sales people, and they always enjoy recognition and challenge, but unfortunately recognition and challenge can't compensate for the accumulated financial equity lost to you in every change of territory. Anticipate this problem by agreeing on a sliding scale of reduced commissions for earlier sales efforts. Twenty-five percent of previous territory commissions for 180 days, and ten percent for a further three months, might be agreed on, depending on the circumstances. An arrangement such as this ensures that your financial rewards keep pace with sales generated as a result of your efforts, and that extra commission costs will make management think twice about moving you.

"Equity drain" is the main reason that sales people, whose efforts build "start-ups" into conglomerates, still retire poor, so establish the equity principle for yourself before taking the job.

Compensation

Compensation packages can consist of straight salary, salary and commission, either or both of these plus bonuses, or straight commission. (Profit sharing may be added to any pay base.) Salaried sellers opt for security and modest returns; commission sales people risk all for the chance of wealth.

Whenever possible, try for a "draw against commission" (cash advances on anticipated sales), with a provision that any money owed will be forgiven if you reach a certain sales level by a given date. This shows the company that you are serious about succeeding, and, in effect, gives you a chance at a nice little added bonus.

To plan your finances, you must know if commissions are payable "on receipt of order," or if you have to wait for customers to pay. The second arrangement makes you a partner with your employer in slow-pay problems, and means that you and the other sales people may be forced to "lend" the company money for months.

Expenses and Insurance

Whether sales expenses are "per diem" or "actual," try for an advance on expenses, so that you are not, once again, continuously lending the company money—and to lessen the risk of not being repaid if you leave under a cloud. Arrange for reimbursement within 30 days of submission (or within your credit card cycle).

Whenever sales people do product demonstrations or installations, they should make sure of company liability insurance coverage.

Agreement and Close

Don't be afraid to negotiate a businesslike Agreement now, in the knowledge that this will only increase future employers' respect for you, and because once you start work it will be too late.

A company officer's (authorized) signature on the contract signals the Close, and that you've made your first big sale!

Getting Started

A Scots detective-sergeant in Glasgow told me years ago that he could nearly always recognize gang leaders from their tendency to stand by themselves. New sales people, whose efforts to organize a territory and develop a work plan are closely scrutinized, can position themselves for promotion by maintaining a slight distance between themselves and their peers. Don't join in when they complain about their territories and the impossible quotas they've been set, but be known from the start for always presenting the positive side of any question. Whatever the cards you're dealt, play them with a smile and without complaint.

Getting Organized

Resist any pressure to "get out and sell" before you've assembled and organized all the leads, account cards, and other information for your territory. The pro and the amateur separate at this point. Organizing includes the rigourous A, B, and C prioritizing of prospects and existing accounts by sales/profit potential, and their arrangement on a map, priorities indicated.

Selling in so many unfamiliar towns and territories forces one to adopt a systematic and ordered approach, and it still surprises me to see so many otherwise-professional sales people "winging it" as they sell. By prioritizing accounts and leads, and learning and laying out a territory properly, these people could realize perhaps another 500 in-person customer contacts a year, and only they know what this would do for their incomes.

Extrapolation of the 80–20 rule implies that 80 percent of sales will come from only 20 percent of accounts (A's plus some B's), so begin by plotting them on a large-scale territory map. Now link your office, home, or hotel with a (color-coded) line to the first A call, which is then connected to other (serially-numbered) A accounts, in the order allowing the largest number of calls in a day. Use different colors to mark

B and C calls, and don't join them to the A's or to each other.

In working the area, start with and stick to A's, unless you pass close to B's, or have time to fill. C's only make it onto the active list when all other higher priority calls for the day have been covered.

A "planet and satellite" call plan is another very efficient way to work an area. Make two A appointments for the morning, two for the afternoon, and fill-in between these "planetary" meetings with short-notice, phone-in-advance "satellite" calls on other A's, and cold calls on B's and C's.

"No Soliciting!"

"Cold calls have no place in today's professional selling!" The new-image, theoretical sales manager who made this statement certainly believed it, and he heard no arguments from a sales force that much preferred chasing leads to cold-call rejection. But, as I told a recent seminar attendee, who asked what to do when faced with a "NO SOLICITING" sign: "There is really no such thing as a "cold call." Tell anyone who points to the sign and objects when you come knocking, 'I'm not soliciting, I'm here to bring you valuable information, and to find out how I can be of help to your company!' "

Again, with cold calling (if we're going to term it that), we're working the numbers—some you win, many you don't. Admittedly, the value of such drop-ins varies in direct proportion to the difficulty of penetrating to the decision-maker, but they in any event test sellers' courage and ability as no other sales situation can, and they keep them *sharp*! The over-organized, play-it-safe mentality never knows the satisfaction of walking into an account, being greeted by a buyer who could have turned you down on the phone, and making a sale! It doesn't matter that it doesn't happen every time—as these are low-priority, fill-in calls—but when it does, the flavor of triumph lasts a long time! And it is the exceptional seller's duty to be inquiring, to question everything, to constantly collect sales intelligence, and to resist anyone who suggests that he sell by rote.

Topography of Sales

Speaking of maps, a "space" sales woman on San Francisco's mid-peninsula reports that she had long been frustrated when comparing steady sales increases in the eastern (Bay) side of her territory with persistent poor performance in the western (coastal) section.

All attempts to balance results seemed to fail until one day when she stumbled on a magnificent, four-color, three-dimensional topographic map of the whole Bay Area in a stationery shop. With the first sight came the realization that sales along the coast were being distorted and constrained by the Coast Range and a narrow, winding road, both intervening between the two halves of her territory. The same intuitive flash told her that because prospects in the coastal towns felt themselves geographically remote from the Bay, they were inclined to give their advertising to local publications. And because she felt physically separated from them by a time-consuming drive, she let them get away with it. Seeing that the problem on both sides was mainly psychological, she immediately increased her personal visits to these customers, and set up regular, frequent telephone contact with them.

Things have gone very well for her all over her territory for some time, but she still keeps a big Bay Area topo map handy, to remind herself how a crooked road and a few hills can affect sales!

Contact Frequency

On a "Customer Contact Value Scale," telephone calls would rate above letters or faxes, and personal visits above all three. But as time is always a seller's most valuable commodity, and personal calls are so time-consuming and expensive, it is well worth looking at a little-considered fact of customer-contact frequency.

> Provided meetings have been held IRREGU-LARLY, customers questioned after nine to twelve months of SATISFACTORY dealing with a supplier CANNOT SAY OFFHAND HOW MANY TIMES THEY HAVE MET WITH SALES PEOPLE.

For time-management-conscious sellers , this means that by avoiding the "set your watch by him . . . every fourth Tuesday at 9 A.M. sharp" meeting pattern, they can expect to substitute phone calls, faxes, and letters for one or more face-to-face meetings a year. And every meeting saved represents time that can be used to develop other new business.

Revenge of the Bean Counters

Like exotic flowers that bloom only in the few hours between dusk and dawn, leads that constitute the life-

blood of selling often represent only the briefest opportunity to make a sale. And when every advertising-
generated lead costs companies cold cash, it is difficult
to explain the weeks or months delay—from initial
prospect-inquiry to eventual follow-up—that are common in U.S. business.

If this has been your experience, look out for the
corporate bean counters, whose anti-selling mindset
often stems from jealousy of sales peoples' lifestyles
and causes them to withold invaluable sources of new
business until their usefulness has long passed. Fighting the system is usually a bit like wrestling in glue,
but you may be able to find a sympathetic sales ad-
ministration clerk prepared to let you have advance
lead-copies for rapid prioritizing and follow-up.

Too many sales people are forced to reinvent the
wheel day after day in selling to multi-location corporations, their divisions and subsidiaries. Lack of a
system for building buyer-company profiles from call
reports, or for circulating lead information among sellers, results in damaging inefficiencies in selling such
accounts. Failing company action, sales people with
their own PC's can network with peers to exchange
leads while they're still hot.

We Only Sell What We Know

Selling PVC industrial hoses through distributors in
the early 1970s, I noticed that the sales reps with the
most loose hose samples and literature in their car
trunks generally knew least about the line and had the
worst sales. My own initial difficulties in wading through

all that paper to understand the product suggested that they might be having the same problem. So I spent several evenings at our San Francisco headquarters three-hole punching sets of product-flyers, specification and safety-data sheets, sales case histories, and price lists, and binding them into handy clear-cover books. Our sales VP balked a little at the cost, but the enthusiastic reception the books received at distributor sales meetings showed that we were on the right track. Soon, consistent sales improvement and a decline in expensive-to-handle distributor inquiries proved that even the most conservative reps were carrying, and using, these books.

We only ever sell what we know and fully understand. Sales pros recognize this, and make sure to have the information they need readily available, in a form that's easy to use and carry.

Know That Order Cycle

Knowing an industry's order cycle is a key factor in maintaining selling energy long enough to Close the sale. It gives the sales person a realistic "time-goal" and replaces blind stubbornness with educated persistence.

Because customers are generally unaware of the sales significance of this order cycle or selling cycle, they tend to drop their guard in the face of knowledgeable sellers, who redouble their efforts when the competition is giving up, and apply Closing pressure towards the end of the critical time period.

Not knowing how long it should take them to get results can be a real "burr under the saddles" of inexperienced sellers. When management doesn't know either—or knowing, keeps it a secret, unfair pressure on sales people may drive them out when they're on the very verge of succeeding. Order cycles (from first contact to making the sale) vary greatly. Thirty minutes might be about right for door-to-door cutlery, with three years on average for some highway products, and the cycles for oil tankers and weapons systems counted in decades.

For the sake of your morale—and to neutralize the pressure to make a sale, any sale, make finding the realistic order cycle for your products or service a first order of business.

Always Ask for the Order!

Educated persistence will always be the most powerful element in high sales achievement. If it sometimes seems that a key account will never buy, remind yourself that of American sales people:

38% contact buyers once and give up.
23% contact buyers twice and stop.
19% contact buyers three times and stop.
20% contact buyers until they make the sale.

45% ask for order once and give up.
25% ask for order twice and stop.
16% ask for order three times and stop.
14% ask for order until they get it.

At least 80% of sales are made by a bare 20% of sellers.
At least 60% of sales are made after the fifth try.

"Never give up, never, never, never, never!" said Winston Churchill.

Sales Reports or Market Intelligence?

The nineteenth-century American "drummers" who opened a vast, newly-settled country to commerce travelled by steam train, stern-wheeler, and horse-drawn buggy on sales trips that sometimes lasted months. Not always the most upright of citizens, they were known for their drinking, gambling, womanizing, and as unprintable raconteurs. If it is true that manufacturers attempted to control them by requiring regular written reports of their activities, we then have to thank them for that bane of sellers' lives—the Sales Report.

Although selling has since gained respect as a profession demanding talent and tenacity, so-called "sales reporting" has not changed much in the last 100 years. It is still used as a crude control mechanism and is still seen by sales people as time-wasting busywork. They resent having to write reports that are so often filed unread, and that take up valuable selling time. Instinctively they know that the concept of reporting is sound, but that the focus is usually all wrong.

Make a simple name-change, from "sales" or "call" *report* to "sales" or "market" *intelligence*, and new purpose and concentration is immediately injected into the whole reporting function. From now on, see yourself as gathering, during every phone call or meeting, essential intelligence to increase your company's prosperity as it furthers your career.

Renounce the purchasing agent's golf game and

marital problems, and the "good call . . . expect order next time . . ." reporting style, to concentrate on market changes; competitors' new products, services, and pricing; detailed account analysis; and customers' suggestions for product modifications. Think always in terms of how this report will help your company to: 1) design the right products for an ever-changing market; 2) plan their production more efficiently; and 3) bring them to customers more quickly and profitably.

Don't let your reports be "round-filed." Highlight significant observations, and draw attention to them on a special cover sheet. Invite comments on key items, and don't hesitate to resubmit reports if they seem to have disappeared into a "black hole" somewhere in the plant. This attitude towards reporting imparts a sharper meaning to selling, and identifies sellers who have it as potential managers interested in more than just the next commission check.

P.I.G.

The sales–prosperity troika's three elements are Persistence, Information, and *Goals*. Good selling is good management—self-management, account-management and future-time-management—in a word, goal-setting. If you haven't already put down short-, medium-, and long-term sales and career objectives, use this format, which allows for six-month, one-year, and five-year goals that can be regularly updated.

List and set your own career objectives NOW! Review them every day, and revise them at every forward step. Holding ambitions in thought like this can cause them to fulfill themselves almost miraculously!

Goal		6 Mos	1 Yr	5 Yr
Salary/Commission	$	_____	_____	_____
Sales to reach above	$	_____	_____	_____
Position/Title/Own business		_____	_____	_____
Major Career Changes		_____	_____	_____
Further Education		_____	_____	_____
Get To Know (names)		_____	_____	_____
Where I Want To Live		_____	_____	_____
Type of House, Apartment, etc.		_____	_____	_____
Car I'd Like To Drive		_____	_____	_____
Ways My Prosperity Will Help To Enrich Others		_____	_____	_____
Other		_____	_____	_____

Winning Actions and Attitudes

- **Use the Seven Steps to sell yourself; then set yourself apart.**
- **Organize, plan, prioritize, and *know* your territory.**
- **Enjoy the adventure of cold calling!**
- **We only sell what we know and understand.**
- **Market Intelligence—not "Sales Reports."**
- **Persistence—Information—Goals, Goals, Goals!!!**

YOUR LIFETIME
SELLING PLAN

In the first chapter of this book, on achieving maximum success in professional selling, we talked about building self-confidence and self-esteem through the powerful, positive affirmations of the Seven Pillars. In this concluding section, let's add to them those indispensable personal qualities and business standards that make for truly happy people who prosper in life as well as in selling.

Professional sales people need pass no stringent examinations, nor hold licences to practice, and this absence of official regulation sometimes leads to their work being seen as a career of last resort. "Selling is easy!", outsiders say, "Anyone can sell!"

But, high-achievement career-selling is not easy! It is different because its fine points must be learned in the University of Life, rather than in conventional schools, and because lifelong dedication is called for in acquiring a wide range of needed professional accomplishments.

Uncommon Talents

Daily personal dealings with all kinds of people teaches sales pros to become polished actors, diplomats, listeners, and communicators, whose appearance and social poise complement their ability to sell. They must also combine complete honesty with a sure-footed capacity to walk the precarious tightrope between customer and "company" interests, while retaining the confidence of both.

Competition for their loyalties, and the need to please everyone all the time, produces people who are forever weighing the odds; who smile a lot while carefully concealing their true feelings; and who are, incidentally, the easiest people in the world to sell. They are past masters at forging seemingly impossible accommodations between suppliers and buyers, but may react to the work pressures by being very hard to live with.

Why, when selling offers exciting, well-paid careers and easy paths to top management, should its practitioners have high rates of divorce and alcoholism, and endure endemic feelings of inadequacy and insecurity? Perhaps because they are so concerned with material success that they haven't found time to confront and bring into balance the conflicting forces in their lives.

Special Responsibilities

Unlike the majority of corporate employees, whose consciences are troubled by nothing worse than the honesty of running personal letters through the office postage meter, sooner or later the majority of sellers have to face serious questions of business morality. As a company's ambassadors to the outside world, how they answer these questions has more than passing significance. The wiser ones come quickly to terms with the ethical choices. Others temporize, make wrong decisions, and sometimes forfeit everything hard work and talent have earned them.

When I was a young and inexperienced salesman,

temptation came my way as "the thing to do"—because "everyone else does it," and ultimately taught me a severe lesson at just the right time. Fortunately, there are watersheds in all our lives, and for me my arrival in America inspired the decision to make a complete break with the past. To remind myself of this resolution, I wrote my "Five Rules For Selling," and have sold and lived by them every since.

The Five Rules

1. I will only sell *honest* goods and services for honest companies. I will be truthful with my company and customers, no matter what the cost. My honest reputation is worth far more to me than any sale.
2. When customers trust me with *confidential* information, I will honor that trust, regardless of pressures to do otherwise. I won't profit from any information to which I don't have honest access. If I'm not entitled to it, I'm better off without it.
3. I will offer *no bribes* and will not try to influence buyers dishonestly in any way.
4. I will take full *responsibility* for all my actions and will not be afraid to face up to my mistakes.
5. I will always set a good *example* to subordinates and will not encourage or condone in others anything I wouldn't do myself.

In the beginning, the harder I clung to the Five Rules, the worse things went—almost as though this way of selling tempted Providence. Sales dropped disastrously, orders were cancelled en masse, and the best Closes suddenly sprang open again. On the day that I could no longer afford to buy food, my car refused to start and notice of a big rent increase arrived in the mail. However, a bright San Francisco sun was starting to burn early morning fog from Russian Hill's lower slopes as the tow truck roared up from Fisherman's Wharf, and that must have been a good omen because the Italian truck driver literally saved the day!

Down to my last seven dollars and fifty cents, and wondering desperately how to pay for a new battery, I'd hardly noticed him looking around the garage— until there he was giving me "cost" on the battery, and fifty dollars for a battered queen-size bed and a folding Christmas tree. Then he peeled the cash from a huge roll of bills, threw his purchases onto the tow truck, and drove off at high speed, singing loudly.

And that was the turning point. From then on, hard work and a growing reputation for honest selling grew steadily into a career that has brought ample financial rewards, a gratifying level of professional recognition, and the opportunity to help many others design their own highly successful sales careers.

Why should you consider guiding your own selling with the Five Rules? Well, let's look at a few of the benefits they offer.

HONEST selling means that as long as we sell honest products or services with integrity, we'll never have to sell an account twice. Customers will accept our counsel regarding which additional products they should buy to increase their profits, and learn to value us as trusted advisors and friends. Justifiable pride in this achievement soon begins to reinforce our growing feelings of confidence and self-worth, and urges us on to ever-increasing business prosperity.

CONFIDENTIALITY is the quality, above all others, dividing superior sales people from sales "sleazes." As part of their job, sellers befriend clients, and deliberately develop trusting relationships with them. The better they are at this, the sooner customers confide in them. Should they then exploit the information gained for their own advantage? Of course not! And yet, this is everyday behavior for far too many sales people who would vehemently deny that they are unscrupulous.

When a sales person shares a client's most confidential business plans with his fiercest competitors, it's only a little worse than filching rival price quotes by reading them "upside-down" in a P.A.'s presence, or quickly checking every file within reach when she leaves the room for a minute. (The knowledge that some buyers intentionally subvert honest bidding by leaving privileged information where competitors can see it changes nothing.)

That "loose lips not only sink ships" but damage lives and companies as well, was brought home sharply to me after many years in selling when the Executive Vice President for a longstanding southern California account told me, as a friend and in strict confidence, that his firm was for sale. Realizing the importance of this news to my company, I still agonized for hours between loyalty to a customer and that owed to my employer. Eventually, I telephoned to tell our general sales manager, but only after swearing him to secrecy on a stack of Bibles.

The following evening, the VP and the company President were dining together at a Los Angeles restaurant when the owner of another of my accounts sat down uninvited at their table and without warning announced that he'd heard their company was on the block, and that he wanted to buy it.

The VP, in poor health at the time, was overcome with shock at this public betrayal of a secret he had only shared with me the day before, and had to have medical attention.

Yes, my superior broke his word, but he wouldn't have been able to if I had not carried loyalty to an employer too far, and in so doing, betrayed the sacred trust of a customer who was also my friend. Such moral dilemmas don't often arise, but when they do it's best to have decided on your position in advance.

BRIBERY With religion banned from schools, ethics seldom taught, and an "anything goes" attitude prevailing in important areas of government and business, a "corruption culture" can sometimes tempt naive sales people into "buying" orders with gifts and bribes. But, regardless of an employer's policy on influencing customers in this way, stop and consider carefully before getting involved. Sellers may boast that they "own" certain purchasing agents and public officials, without mentioning that this is strictly a two-way street. We may own them, but just as surely, they own us, and who in their right mind really wants to enter into such an infernal marriage contract?

No matter how heartbreaking it is to lose order after order to corrupt competitors, the alternatives are always far worse. Bribery may appear to pay immediate dividends, but an unblemished reputation for honesty guarantees a lifetime of far greater rewards.

RESPONSIBILITY says that we ourselves are always the ultimate arbiters of our values and the course of our lives. Companies can circulate ethical codes and spout platitudes about integrity, honor, and sincerity, but they mean absolutely nothing until employees buy into these concepts of their own volition. As sales people fortify their self-esteem through the Seven Pillars and their sales with the Seven Steps, little by little they find it easier to admit mistakes and take full responsibility for every aspect of their lives. The moment they do so, they are, for the first time, completely free to reach their full potential for happiness and success.

EXAMPLE The best managers lead by example in establishing standards for others that they've already met themselves. As an eventual sales manager or CEO, you will be under occasional pressure to produce results at any cost. Prepare now to demand only the highest standards of yourself and others. Integrity, like truth, is indivisible!

Winning Actions and Attitudes

- **Continuously raise your professionalism, and develop those "uncommon talents."**
- **Learn and live by the Five Rules.**
- **With the signing of a purchase order, THE SELLING HAS ONLY JUST BEGUN!!!**

A Final Word

I have written this book to INSPIRE, MOTIVATE, ENERGIZE and OPEN WIDE WINDOWS-OF-OPPORTUNITY for all those Sales Professionals and would-be Selling Stars who have a job but not a career; or a career that doesn't satisfy.

If you KNOW, deep in your heart, that you can be the BEST, this book shows you how!

APPENDIX I
PERSONAL SALES
SKILLS CHECK LIST

Mark yourself conservatively, on a *RISING 1 to 10 Scale*; allow room for future improvements.

1. How well are you answering the vital question: "What exactly am I selling?" ☐

2. Rate your Sales Motivation & Enjoyment of Selling. ☐

3. How good are your (speaking/writing) Communications Skills? ☐

4. Rate your Linking ability & Comfort-Level when meeting strangers. ☐

5. How committed are you to helping solve Customers' Problems? ☐

6. Rate yourself on selling Value versus Price. ☐

7. How important are Ethics, Integrity, and Trust in selling? ☐

8. Rate your commitment to a high level of Customer Service. ☐

9. How good are you at asking for the order? ☐

10. Time is your most valuable sales commodity. Rate yourself on how well you "Plan your work and work your plan"? ☐

11. How would your customers rate you on Honesty, Appearance, Follow-Up, Product Knowledge, and Service? ☐

12. Of the opportunities open to you, where do you place a career in Sales? ☐

Total ____

Divide by 12 = Average ____

8–10 Avg. indicates high sales professionalism.

5–7 Avg. indicates need for further sales skills training.

2–4 Avg. indicates need to consider other career options.

APPENDIX 2
THE ART OF
PRESENTING YOUR
BUSINESS CARD

Business cards may be the most underused and least understood of all the basic sales resources. Every day, American sales people give out and accept literally millions of cards—almost without a thought. Each of these unthinking transactions is a lost opportunity to impress prospects with valuable information about their companies and themselves.

Of course, your card will show the company name, logo, address and phone number, with name and title, but it should not otherwise be too memorable: Cards that attract much attention distract from the sales call itself. This is well illustrated by one from a salesman at a Los Angeles trade show that read:

> Doc Jones, Sales Representative,
> The ____ Company
> Five Minutes And A Friend For Life!

I worried then, as I often have since, just how many minutes were actually spent with the good Doc, and will he one day track me down and claim me for his lifelong friend? But I have no idea what he was selling!

Cards with corners bent from being kept in over-stuffed wallets and cheap plastic cases are part of a general carelessness in carrying and presenting them.

From the Nov./Dec. 1986 issue of *Personal Selling Power*, p. 1.

A friend of mine was even asked to return a warped and grubby card that also happened to have the family shopping list written on the back.

By contrast, those master sales people, the Japanese, attach great importance to business cards and the ways in which they are carried and presented. After all, it was Japan Airlines that initiated the printing of bilingual business cards in time for the arrival of their Tokyo-bound first-class passengers.

In listing some rules for business card etiquette, Japan's Modern Communications Centre says that cards should be informative rather than gaudy, and frowns on some of the more colorful American ones. A favorite from my collection shows the 'hang ten' outline of a huge pair of feet, though displaying various parts of the human anatomy in this way could easily get out of hand.

The M.C.C. also insists that cards be carried in well-made silk or leather cases, and in an outside pocket, as no one like to be given a warm, damp card. The modern Japanese business person would no more make sales calls without an ample supply of "meishi" (business cards) than a Samurai would go to war without his sword. To run out of cards and then make feeble cover-up excuses is just "not done" in Japan.

Just as Western business cards trace their origins to nineteenth-century social calling cards, which were received at the front door by a servant with a special tray, so the Japanese observe strict protocol in presenting a card. They believe that it should always be offered and accepted while standing, and it is the height of good manners to receive it with both hands.

There's no need for excessive formality in exchanging cards here, but extract the greatest advantage from the transaction by thinking of your card as an item of value, and waiting for the right moment to present it.

There is often a natural pause in the conversation, somewhere at the start of a sales call, and perhaps just after you have been asked to sit down. This can be the perfect time to take out your card. Remain standing, look the prospect in the eye, and as you present your card, repeat your name clearly and distinctly, even if you have only recently introduced yourself.

This will leave an enduring impression of your appearance and your name, linked to that of your company and its logo, as recipients meet your gaze and hear your name before instinctively glancing down at the card. It also puts them at ease by letting them use your name with confidence when they may have misheard or quickly forgotten it.

At this point, if you are not offered a card in return, ask for one. Don't do any selling until the exchange has been completed. By remaining standing, and asking for a card in return, you have begun to control the meeting at its outset, and can build on this advantage to complete the sale.

When someone doesn't have a card, don't be embarrassed to ask for the same information on a piece of paper, while stressing how important correct names and titles are to you. This reassures prospects that you will be just as careful with the vital details of their orders.

Sales people who don't bother to ask for cards constantly miss chances to demonstrate their professionalism, to control the sales encounter, and to show that they care about those all-important details. They also forget that to customers, the most welcome words of all are their own names correctly pronounced and spelled.

So the next time you prepare for a day's sales calls, make sure to include a liberal supply of those great little billboards—your business cards.

APPENDIX 3
A ROUND-UP OF
FORMS

Most sales departments use some variations of the forms in this round-up. Sales newcomers and newly appointed sales managers will want to look at these examples. Remember that, although there are no such things as "good" forms, properly used, forms still complete a well-rounded management package.

Account Card 1, Side A

GRAPHIC PRODUCTS
PERMANENT ACCOUNT RECORD

COMPANY _____
SIC CODE _____
ADDRESS _____
CITY, STATE, ZIP _____
CONTACT(S) _____
TITLE _____
PHONE _____
DEPT. _____
LOCATION _____

ACCOUNT# _____

TARGET TRACKING CODE _____

CONTACT(S)/PERSONAL DETAILS
_____
_____
_____

COMPANY STRUCTURE
NO. OF EMPLOYEES _____ ANN. SALES VOL.$ _____
COMPETITORS _____
DECISION MAKING PROCESS/ INDIVIDUALS
_____
_____
_____
_____
_____
_____

DIVISION/AFFILIATION/PARENT _____

Account Card 1, Side B

COMPANY MISSION _____
_____ _____
ANNUAL PURCHASES OF OUR PROD/SVC
DOLLARS_____UNITS_____
BUYING DECISIONS BASED ON:
☐ QUALITY ☐ PRICE ☐ DELIVERY
OTHER MAJOR BUYING LOCATIONS AND
CONTACT NAMES_____
_____
_____
_____
_____

PROD/SVC PURCHASED FOR
☐ INTERNAL USE ☐ RESALE ☐ EXPORT
PROD/SVC PURCHASED ON A
☐ PROGRAM BASIS ☐ PROJECT BASIS
SALES TAX EXEMPT?
☐ YES   ☐ NO
OTHER PROD/SVC WE COULD SELL THIS
ACCOUNT
_____
_____
_____
D&B NO._____

COMPETING SUPPLIER(S)_____
PRODUCT(S)/SERVICE(S)_____
SPECIAL CAPABILITIES_____
DECORATION_____
PRICES _____
DATE LAST ORDERED _____ORDER FREQUENCY _____

ADDITIONAL INFORMATION _____
_____

COMPETITIVE DATA

Account Card 2, Sides C & D

DATE	CALL SUMMARY	FOLLOW-UP DATE

ACCOUNT ACTIVITY LOG:
COMPANY_____
ACCOUNT#_____

YEAR   SALES PLANNING CONTROL SHEET   **SALESPERSON**

O = Home Office
□ = Plant or Branch
△ = Purchasing

P = Phone Call
L = Letter
V = Visit
F = Fax
I = First Order

ACCOUNT PRIORITY	ESTD CONTACTS PER YR	CUSTOMER	JANUARY	FEBRUARY	MARCH	APRIL	MAY	JUNE	JULY	AUGUST	SEPTEMBER	OCTOBER	NOVEMBER	DECEMBER	TOTAL CONTACTS
A	12	Aardvark Advertising □	P P P	P	P	V	P	P	V	P	P	V	L L	P	14
A	16	Bedrock Mattress △	V	V	P	V!	P	P	V	P	P		L		13
A	15	Cedilla Services O		L	P!	P	L	P		P	L	F		L	11
A	10	Drongo I.Q. Testing △		P	P				V	P	P		V		19
A	6	Easterly Aircraft Parts □		P!	P	F	P		P	V!	V	F	P	L	11
B	8	Andic Hay & Feed O		V	V	P!	P	P			V	P	P	P	8
B	7	Disparate Weights △	L		P		P		L! P	P	V		P	P	10
B	8	E&S Steam Supply O			P	P	V		V		P		V		6
B	6	Lingua Franka Salami O		F		L		P	P!		P				6
C	5	Chatterbox Records □		V						V!					4
C	4	Dorothy Matrix Inc. □					V			L	P		P	P	4
C	2	Cucaracha Pest Control □	P			P	P								3

Planning Sheet

Sales Report

SALES INTELLIGENCE REPORT W/O 2 15 90 SALESPERSON E. King PAGE NO. 3/5

DATE OF CALL	ACCOUNT AND LOCATION	CONTACT	DETAILS OF CALL	ACTION	REF
2/6	Cucaracha 63 Shanti St.	Barry Tell	Business Better. Buying Out Anterior Exterminators, Inc. This means New Buying Locations in (our) territories 'D','F' and 'R' (Contacts (phone #s encl.) Meese's Pest Powder Now 10% Higher than us. Cucaracha sees steady 5-7% P.A. increase in purchase of our products for 5 years.	Quote Barry 3/15 on Appl. Equipt.	2/88
2/6	Bedrock Mattress 1 Queens Road	Eliz. Valance	Tighter Fed Regulations will force Bedrock to drop the special-order deodorant they buy from us by 3/92. This gives us time to develop an alternative product. Orders of present product will stay at current levels until 12/91	Arrange meeting between our chemists and their production people	4/89
2/7	Andic Hay and Feed Box 37, RR 2	Bill Grist	Competitor's Feed Additive superior to ours at lower cost. He's under pressure to change sources.	Consider lower cost re-formulation	10/89

Prospective Business Report

ACCT/DIST MGR _E. King_   MONTH/YR _3-90_

SALESPERSON'S MONTHLY PROSPECTIVE BUSINESS REPORT

PROSPECT	SALES $ POTENTIAL	SPECIFIC PRODUCTS	FOLLOW-UP SEQUENCE	COMMENTS
Bedrock Mattress	70 m P.A.	Deodorants	Every 4 weeks on average	See S.I.R. 2/6
Andic H&F	35 m -0-	low cost additive	phone/visit 8 week average	-0- 2/6
Cucaracha	92 m - 0-	Misc. Chemicals	phone/letter 16 week average	-0- 2/7

Telephone Sales Report

Daily Phone Prospecting Activity

Salesperson _____   Date: _____

No. of Attempts _____   No. of Contacts _____

	NAME	COMPANY	RESULT
1.			
2.			
3.			
4.			
5.			

Questions I could not answer _____

Summary:

Proposal Blank

PROPOSAL

ALMOND BINDER PRODUCTS

DATE *Sept. 4, 1990*

Page No. *one*   Pages *one*

PROPOSAL SUBMITTED TO (COMPANY)
Aadvaark Advertising

CONTACT   PHONE( )
Rob Dent

STREET
Terminus Place

CITY   STATE   ZIP

SHIP TO (COMPANY)
Aadvaark

CONTACT   PHONE
R. Dent

STREET

CITY   STATE   ZIP

We hereby propose to furnish materials and labor necessary for the completion of:

Four thousand five hundred, three inch overlay
Binders (white with red logo, per approved artwork)
Special, heavy-duty metals (per customer sample supplied)

FOB
☐ DESTINATION   ☑ PREPAY
☑ PLANT   ☐ COLLECT

TAX
EXEMPT
☐ YES # _____
☑ NO

ADD'L
CHARGES
☑ ARTWORK   ☐ DIE
☑ SCREEN   ☐ OTHER

PAYMENT
TERMS
NET

WE PROPOSE hereby to furnish material and labor — complete in accordance with above specifications, for the sum of:

thirty five thousand, two hundred and thirty five $^{nil}/_{100}$ dollars ($ *35,235* $^{00}/_{100}$)

Payment to be made as follows:
50% deposit in two weeks ; balance prior to shipment

All material is guaranteed to be as specified. All work to be completed in a substantial workmanlike manner according to specifications submitted, per standard practices. Any alteration or deviation from above specifications involving extra costs will be executed only upon written orders, and will become an extra charge over and above the estimate. All agreements contingent upon strikes, accidents or delays beyond our control. Owner to carry fire, tornado and other necessary insurance. Our workers are fully covered by Workmen's Compensation Insurance.

Authorized
Signature _____

Note: This proposal may be
withdrawn by us if not accepted within 30 days.

ACCEPTANCE OF PROPOSAL The above prices, specifications and conditions are satisfactory and are hereby accepted. You are authorized to do the work as specified. Payment will be made as outlined above.

Authorized
Signature *Authorized*   title: _____

Date of Acceptance: _____

Authorized
Signature *Authorized*   title: _____

Credit Application

Consumer Chemical Corp.

Account Credit Statement

Company Name _____ Telephone _____

Street Address _____

Mailing Address (if different) _____

City _____ State _____ Zip Code _____

Organization Information:

     Subsidiary or Division of _____

     Date Business Started _____

     Nature of Business _____

     Chief Executive Officer _____

     Chief Financial Officer _____

     Accounts Payable Contact _____

Trade References:

     Name _____ Telephone _____

     Street Address _____

     City _____ State _____ Zip Code _____

     Name _____ Telephone _____

     Street Address _____

     City _____ State _____ Zip Code _____

     Name _____ Telephone _____

     Street Address _____

     City _____ State _____ Zip Code _____

Bank Reference:

     Name _____ Telephone _____

     Street Address _____

     City _____ State _____ Zip Code _____

     Contact _____ Account Number _____

Sales and Use Taxes:

     If the items purchased from Consumer Chemical Corp. are not subject to sales and use taxes, please complete the Sales Tax Exemption Certificate on the reverse side of this form.

Signature _____

Date _____ Title _____

Sales Order

CONSUMER CHEMICAL CORP.

ORDER FORM

ORDER DATE:	CUSTOMER ORDER NUMBER:

SOLD TO:
Bedrock Mattress MFG.
1 Queens Road

SHIP TO:
1 Queens Road

see : Danny
TELEPHONE: _(910) 243 - 4321_

DATE REQUIRED: _5-15. - 9_   TERMS: _Net 2% -30Days_   F.O.B.: _Peoria Plant_

SALESPERSON: FOR OFFICE USE ONLY:

QUANTITY	DESCRIPTION	UNIT PRICE		TOTAL	
150	～ ～ ～ ～	83	90	12,585	00

Change Order

TO: ☐ **ALMOND BINDER PRODUCTS**

CHANGE ORDER

VERBAL CHANGES MUST BE CONFIRMED IN WRITING AND MAILED SAME DATE

COMPANY NAME: _____   DATE: _____

ADDRESS   : _____   CUSTOMER P.O. NO.: _____

_____   DATE OF P.O.: _____

_____   OUR JOB NO.: _____

NAME OF SALESPERSON: _____   SALESPERSON NO.: _____

CHANGE WAS MADE BY PHONE: ☐ YES ☐ NO   DATE _____   CONTACT: _____

DESCRIPTION OF PRODUCT: _____

_____

DESCRIPTION OF CHANGE: _____

_____

_____

_____

_____

_____

_____

_____

_____

_____

_____

_____

ADDITIONAL CHARGES: _____

_____   _____

SALESPERSON'S SIGNATURE   DATE

USE SECOND FORM IF ADDITIONAL SPACE IS REQUIRED.

SALESMAN IS RESPONSIBLE FOR ALL ERRORS IF NOT CONFIRMED IN WRITING.

SALES SERVICE COPY